GUERRILLAS
—IN—
CIVIL WAR
MISSOURI

JAMES W. ERWIN

THE
History
PRESS

Published by The History Press
Charleston, SC 29403
www.historypress.net

Front cover: Quantrill's Guerrillas, Missouri Partizan Rangers, 1863, by Don Troiani.
www.historicalimagebank.com.
Back cover: Martial Law, or Order No.11, by George Caleb Bingham. *From the Art Collection, The
State Historical Society of Missouri, Columbia.*

First published 2012

ISBN 978-1-5402-0626-8

Library of Congress Cataloging-in-Publication Data
Erwin, James W.
Guerrillas in Civil War Missouri / James W. Erwin.
p. cm.
Includes bibliographical references and index.
ISBN 978-1-60949-388-2
1. Missouri--History--Civil War, 1861-1865--Underground movements. 2. Missouri-
-History--Civil War, 1861-1865--Commando operations. 3. Missouri--History--Civil
War, 1861-1865--Campaigns. 4. Guerrilla warfare--Missouri--History--19th century. 5.
Guerrillas--Missouri--History--19th century. I. Title.
E470.45.E78 2012
977.8'03--dc23
2011050227

Contents

CONTENTS

Preface

During the Civil War, Missouri was in constant turmoil from raids by heavily armed bands of marauders loosely affiliated with the Confederate army. Federal troops fought more than one thousand battles in Missouri—mostly with these guerrillas. But the numbers mask the level of violence because they do not include attacks on civilians. Ordinary persons felt the dread of uncertainty when riders approached their homes. Were they Union soldiers or guerrillas in blue coats taken off soldiers they had ambushed? Sometimes it did not matter. Either side might kill the men and burn their buildings if dissatisfied with the response to their demands for information, food or horses. Entire counties were reduced to ruins.

A Civil War cliché is that the war pitted brother against brother. No doubt that must have happened, but Missouri's civil war was personal on another level. As General John Pope wrote, it was a frequent occurrence for a party of "bushwhackers…with fierce oaths and loud threats of burning his house" to demand that a man or (more likely during the war) his wife provide food, horses and money. The guerrillas and their victims were not strangers. They were neighbors from the family down the road. And the guerrillas' families could expect the same treatment from other neighbors who were members of the Missouri militia or, worse, Jayhawkers from Kansas.

There were few set-piece battles in Missouri. It was left to the armies in the other theaters to provide the dramatic charges and heroic defenses. In Missouri, a soldier may be shot riding down a seemingly peaceful road. A guerrilla unlucky enough to be captured would somehow always be reported as shot "trying to escape."

After the war, the former antagonists debated who was responsible for the escalating cycle of killing, retribution and revenge that became ever more savage as the war continued. Who was the first to scalp the dead enemy? Who was the first to mutilate the bodies of the dead? Once it began, however, the origins no longer mattered. Postwar author John N. Edwards wrote of Jesse James—but it could have been applied to any man caught up in the guerrilla war—"He did what he did. But it was war."

This was Missouri's guerrilla war: a war of retaliation, savagery and few prisoners.

Acknowledgements

My debt to the historians listed in the bibliography is evident. I hope that this introduction to the guerrilla war in Missouri will make the reader want to learn more about the subjects these authors have explored in depth.

I want to acknowledge the assistance of Sara Przybylski at the State Historical Society of Missouri at Columbia, Missouri, and Dorris Keeven-Franke at the St. Charles Historical Society for their help in obtaining photographs and illustrations for this book. I also want to thank Colter Sikora for the excellent maps.

Finally, I must give the most credit to my wife, Vicki. Without her encouragement, suggestions and, yes, prodding, this book would never have been conceived, let alone completed. Thanks, Vicki, I love you.

Missouri R.

Platte R.

DEKALB

DONIPHAN

St. Joseph

Hannibal & St. Joseph RR

Easton

BUCHANAN

CLINTON

CALDWELL

ATCHISON

PLATTE

RAY

Leavenworth

CLAY

Liberty

Albany

Missouri R.

JEFFERSON

LEAVENWORTH

Kansas City

Sibley

Lexington

WYANDOTTE

Kansas R.

Independence

LAFAYETTE

Lecompton

Kansas R.

Westport

Lawrence

JACKSON

Wakarusa R.

JOHNSON

Lone Jack

DOUGLAS

Aubry

Warrensburg

FRANKLIN

MIAMI

Pleasant Hill

Marais des Cygnes R.

Paola

Harrisonville

JOHNSON

Osawatomie

CASS

Osage R.

Pottawatomie Cr.

BATES

HENRY

Trading Post

Butler

ANDERSON

LINN

ST. CLAIR

Osage R.

Osceloa

ALLEN

BOURBON

Marmaton R.

Nevada City

Ft. Scott

VERNON

CEDAR

NEOSHO

CRAWFORD

K A N S A S

M I S S O U R I

Lamar

BARTON

DADE

LABETTE

CHEROKEE

Osage R.

LAWRENCE

Ft. Blair
(Baxter Springs)

JASPER

Kansas

AREA OF
DETAIL

Missouri

0   10   20 mi

0   10   20 km

N

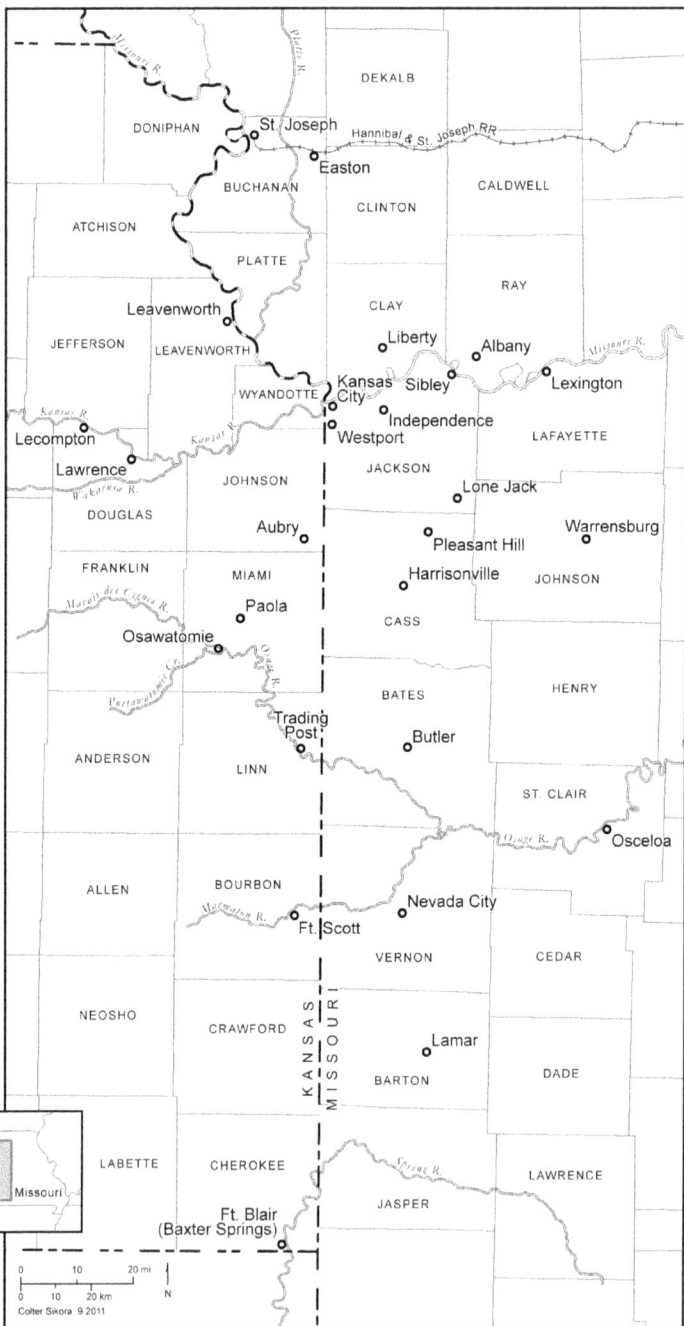

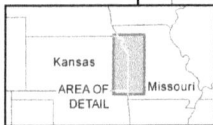

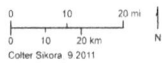

Colter Sikora 9.2011

Above: North central and northeastern Missouri. Little Dixie extended from Callaway County on both sides of the Missouri River to Jackson County. *Map by Colter Sikora.*

Opposite: Western Missouri and eastern Kansas. The area affected by Order No. 11 was Jackson, Cass, Bates and the northern third of Vernon Counties. Most of Missouri's slaves lived in "Little Dixie," the counties along the Missouri River. *Map by Colter Sikora.*

Chapter 1

The War Before the War

THE KANSAS-NEBRASKA ACT

The roots of the guerrilla war in Missouri—like the Civil War itself—can be traced to the issue of slavery in the territories.

Missouri was part of the Louisiana Purchase. While the state's application to become a state was pending, Alabama was admitted as a slave state, making the number of slave and free states equal. The impasse was broken by an agreement to admit Missouri as a slave state and Maine as a free state. The Missouri Compromise settled the question of allowing slavery in states created from the Louisiana Territory, at least for the time being, by prohibiting it north of the 36°30' parallel, the southern boundary of Missouri.

Few were satisfied, but the arrangement maintained sectional balance and kept the question of slavery in newly acquired lands from further dividing the country. Thomas Jefferson rightly considered that the slavery issue was "hushed indeed for the moment, but this is a reprieve only, not a final sentence. [A] geographical line, coinciding with a marked principle, moral and political, once conceived and held up to the angry passions of men, will never be obliterated; and every new irritation will mark it deeper and deeper."

And indeed, the question of the extension of slavery erupted after the United States again acquired considerable territory, this time as a result of the Mexican War. The dispute raged for four years until Congress approved the Compromise of 1850. Under this agreement, Texas was admitted to

Illinois senator Stephen A. Douglas, author of the Kansas-Nebraska Act of 1854 and Democratic candidate for president in 1860. *Library of Congress.*

the Union, all of California (even the part south of the 36°30' parallel) was admitted as a free state, a stronger Fugitive Slave Act was passed and slavery was preserved in the District of Columbia. But the Compromise of 1850 was doomed to last only four years.

Senator Stephen A. Douglas thought he had the solution to the political turmoil that had racked the country for decades over slavery and threatened to divide his Democratic Party: popular sovereignty. Let the people decide. In January 1854, he introduced the Kansas-Nebraska Act, which proclaimed that "the questions pertaining to slavery in the territories, and in the new states to be formed therefrom, are to be left to the decision of the people residing therein, through their representatives."

The Kansas-Nebraska Act repealed the Missouri Compromise and threatened to undo the Compromise of 1850. Rather than solve the problem of the extension of slavery to the territories, however, it made it worse. Immediately after the bill was introduced, Northern antislavery politicians condemned it as "a gross violation of a sacred pledge; as a criminal betrayal of precious rights; as part and parcel of an atrocious plot to exclude from a vast unoccupied region immigrants from the Old World and free laborers from our own States, and convert it into a dreary region of despotism, inhabited by masters and slaves." Thomas Hart Benton, the former longtime senator from Missouri, now a representative from St. Louis, attacked the bill's repeal of the Missouri Compromise, declaring that he "had stood upon [the agreement]…above thirty years, and intended to stand upon it to the end—solitary and alone, if need be; but preferring company." But Congress approved the bill, narrowly in the House and by a greater margin in the Senate. President Franklin Pierce signed the act into law on May 30, 1854.

Senator William Seward of New York, speaking for the antislavery advocates, accepted the slave states' challenge "on behalf of the cause of freedom. We will engage in competition for the virgin soil of Kansas, and God give the victory to the side that is stronger in numbers as it is in right."

BLEEDING KANSAS:
JAYHAWKERS AND BORDER RUFFIANS

And where popular sovereignty was the rule, numbers were power. Both sides recognized that quickly.

Northern antislavery activists organized companies, such as the Massachusetts Emigrant Aid Society (later the New England Emigrant

Aid Society), to claim Kansas as a free state. The first such group arrived in Kansas on July 17, 1854, led by (among others) Daniel B. Anthony (Susan B. Anthony's brother). They found a beautiful spot overlooking the Kaw River that they named Mount Oread (now the site of the University of Kansas). The city of Lawrence was laid out at its foot. Six groups of settlers sponsored by the society arrived that summer—about six hundred persons overall.

Proslavery adherents, however, had the advantage because they could merely cross over from Missouri to stake their claims. Leavenworth, initially a proslavery town, was founded by Missourians within two weeks of the signing of the Kansas-Nebraska Act into law. Many Missouri settlers long coveted the area and were able to claim the most desirable land before those from the east could get their bearings.

More than politics divided the northeastern emigrants from those from western Missouri. The New Englanders regarded themselves as superior to the westerners, not just because they supported a system that in their view rewarded hard work versus one that racially stigmatized labor but also because the westerners were crude and uncouth "pukes."

Missourians returned the contempt. They chortled when many northeastern settlers found life in Kansas too hard and went back to more congenial circumstances. These northerners were, as one newspaper put it, "mostly ignorant of agriculture, picked up in cities and villages, they of course have no experience as farmers, and if left to their unaided resources—if not clothed and fed by the same power which has effected their transportation—they would starve."

Not all of the free-soil settlers were from New England or the beneficiaries of the Emigrant Aid Societies. Indeed, most came from the Ohio Valley—Illinois, Indiana and Ohio. But the northeasterners, while making up less than 5 percent of the antislavery settlers, were the most vocal and influential.

Although the territory's governor, Andrew Reeder, declared that only "residents" could vote in Kansas's first election for its delegate to Congress, the two sides squared off on the definition of residence—did one have to prove he actually lived in Kansas or only intended to do so? In any event, it didn't matter what the governor said. J.W. Whitfield, late of Jackson County, Missouri, won with 2,258 of 2,833 votes cast, including an estimated 1,700 from Missourians who showed up the night before the election.

The March 1855 election for the first territorial legislature had a similar outcome. This time, the proslavery Missourians sent an armed force to ensure the result. Newspaperman Horace Greeley dubbed these men "Border Ruffians." Their political opponents derided them as a

lawless mob...drunken, bellowing, blood thirsty demons...for the most part of large frame, with red flannel shirts and immense boots worn outside their trousers, their faces unwashed and unshaven...wearing the most savage looks and giving utterance to the most horrible imprecations and blasphemies; armed, moreover, to the teeth with rifles, revolvers, cutlasses and bowie-knives.

But many were, in fact, leading citizens of Missouri. Missouri senator David Rice Atchison was the most prominent Border Ruffian. He was one of a group of proslavery senators who helped Douglas get the Kansas-Nebraska Act passed. Although Atchison may have owned only one slave (the record is unclear), he was a strong proponent of slavery. He embraced the nickname Border Ruffians, declaring them to be "men of property, of education—the best kind of men. We are the men who will submit to no wrong."

Claiborne Fox Jackson was another Border Ruffian of property and education. He was a lawyer who, after serving in the militia in the Black Hawk War of 1832, opened a store in Arrow Rock, Saline County. There, Jackson met and married the youngest of Dr. John Sappington's three daughters. Sappington was a wealthy and influential planter who numbered President Andrew Jackson and Thomas Hart Benton among his friends. When Jackson's first wife died, he married the oldest Sappington daughter. She died as well, and Jackson married the middle daughter. Dr. Sappington

Missouri senator David Rice Atchison. Atchison was an ardent proslavery advocate. He helped pass the Kansas-Nebraska Act of 1854 and was a leader of the Border Ruffians. Photograph by Mathew B. Brady, March 1849. *General Collection, Beinecke Rare Book and Manuscript Library, Yale University.*

was supposed to have grudgingly agreed to the third marriage, muttering, "You can take her, but don't come back after the old woman."

Jackson's father-in-law gave him an entrée into Missouri politics. In the 1840s, he became a member of Benton's "Central Clique" that controlled the Democratic Party in the state and served twelve years in the legislature. By 1850, however, he had broken with Benton over the issue of slavery. Jackson's most visible act was to sponsor a series of resolutions declaring that Congress had no right to decide whether any territory would be slave or free.

Claiborne Fox Jackson. Jackson was a leader of the Border Ruffians. Elected governor of Missouri in 1860, he tried unsuccessfully to have the state join the Confederacy in 1861. *The State Historical Society of Missouri, Columbia.*

Missourians had their own derogatory term for antislavery partisans— "Jayhawkers." The origin of the term is unclear, but to proslavery forces, it came to signify Kansans who murdered Missourians and slave owners and burned and looted their property, all in the name of "freedom" for the black man.

For the March 1855 election to choose the first territorial legislature, Governor Reeder had a census taken to minimize voter fraud. Although the census found only 2,905 eligible voters, 6,307 votes were cast, most of them by Missourians led by Atchison and Jackson, who arrived the night before. Not surprisingly, all but 900 votes went to proslavery candidates. Reeder voided the results in several districts and required another vote. This time, free-soil candidates won. But when the legislature met at Lecompton, it threw out the results of the second election and seated the proslavery candidates.

Having no success in obtaining fair elections, the free-soilers decided to form their own state government. They met in Topeka in late 1855. The Topeka convention drafted its own constitution that prohibited slavery. In January 1856, the free-soilers elected Charles Robinson their governor. Curiously, the Topeka government was no friendlier to African Americans than the Lecompton government. Most of those voting for the Topeka government were not abolitionists. Indeed, apart from Robinson and his more vocal supporters, the free-soilers "warred not against slavery in the abstract, only slavery in Kansas." Even the Topeka free-soil constitution prohibited *both* slaves and free blacks from settling in the territory. The Kansas free-soilers generally "hate slavery but they hate the Negro worse," noted Samuel Adair, an antislavery minister. "The ignorance of some of these men is most profound."

The years 1855–56 gave the name "Bleeding Kansas" to the prewar events on the border. The violence began over land claims, not politics. In the rush to settle Kansas, the government had not yet completely surveyed the state. Antislavery Charles Dow and proslavery Franklin Coleman clashed over a 250-yard strip of ground in Douglas County. The dispute grew tense until, on November 21, Coleman shot and killed Dow. Sheriff Samuel Jones arrested Jacob Branson, a friend of Dow's, for allegedly threatening retaliation against Coleman. A band of antislavery men rescued Branson and took him to Lawrence for protection. Jones's call for help was answered by hundreds of Border Ruffians led by David Atchison. They squared off against antislavery forces for two weeks before both sides dispersed.

But new names were introduced to the Kansans that were to play a leading role in subsequent events: James H. Lane and John Brown.

Lane commanded an Indiana regiment in the Mexican War and was elected the state's lieutenant governor twice before moving to Kansas in 1855. He would later become a leading Kansas Jayhawker, its first senator and a Union general. Historian George Fort Milton described Lane as "poorly educated, coarse and uncouth. His hair stood out in every direction, his mouth suggested plug tobacco and heavy curses and his dress was almost as extraordinary as his appearance. But this was not all of the man. Positive, insistent, domineering and dominant, he commanded his fellows. His energy was amazing." Lane was a charismatic speaker, with what Donald Gilmore described as a "bizarre, rasping, affected voice, punctuated throughout by audible gasps of air."

Born in Connecticut, Brown also migrated to Kansas in 1855. He was involved in the Underground Railroad in the Midwest and sought "to help defeat SATAN and his legions" in his new home. Within weeks, he became a captain in the antislavery forces. He was disappointed when that fall's confrontation fizzled out. But there would be other opportunities.

Sporadic violence over the next few months erupted into something much more serious in May 1856. Sheriff Jones was shot and wounded early in the month. A grand jury dominated by proslavery men indicted several free-state leaders on rather flimsy evidence. On May 21, United States marshal Israel Donalson rode to Lawrence to arrest them, backed

James H. Lane. Lane was a leader of the Kansas abolitionists, one of the first senators from the state when it joined the Union in 1861 and a Union brigadier general. He was a notorious Jayhawker who, early in the Civil War, led raids on western Missouri. *Library of Congress*.

John Brown. Brown was the leader of the Potawatomie Massacre in 1856 that initiated the round of violence that gave Bleeding Kansas its name. *Library of Congress.*

by some eight hundred Missourians again led by David Atchison. This time, the confrontation did not end peaceably. After the marshal made the arrest, Atchison's Border Ruffians burned the Free State Hotel, destroyed two abolitionist newspapers and threw their type into the river.

Bloody retaliation was not long in coming. On the night of May 24, John Brown, three of his sons and four other men approached the cabin of James Doyle, a proslavery man, near Pottawatomie, Kansas. The raiders took Doyle and two of his sons into the night. Later, they seized Allen Wilkinson, a member of the proslavery legislature. At the house of James Harris, the attackers questioned the owner and two travelers who were staying the night. One of the men, William Sherman, was determined to be proslavery; the others were not and were released. Sherman, however, was taken away.

Brown and his men murdered the five captives. The Doyles were hacked to death with swords. The youngest had his arms cut off. Wilkinson's throat was cut. Sherman was found in a creek, his skull split open in two places and his brains spilling into the water and his left hand cut off. Brown never directly admitted to participating in what became known as the Pottawatomie Massacre. When pressed about his involvement by one of his sons who was not on the raid, the most Brown would say was, "God is my judge. We were justified under the circumstances."

The massacre set off a round of retaliatory violence that presaged the border depredations by both sides in the Civil War. In June, Brown and his men met a group of Missourians under St. Louis newspaperman Henry Pate in the Battle of Black Jack. Brown's men surrounded Pate and, after an exchange of gunfire, demanded his surrender. Pate, convinced he was outnumbered, gave up. "I went to take Old Brown," he later said, "and he took me." Shortly afterward, Federal troops from Fort Leavenworth appeared and forced Brown to release his prisoners. They also dispersed a larger Missouri force that was coming to attack Brown.

David Atchison ordered the border between Missouri and Kansas closed. Antislavery partisans seeking to cross the Missouri River were turned back. But Lane, who had been back east, was returning with an army through Nebraska. Proslavery partisans in Leavenworth and northern Kansas were thrown into a panic.

Free-soil forces attacked several proslavery Kansas outposts in August. In what would become a familiar scene a few years later, the victors plundered the vanquished's homes. Proslavery Henry Titus offered a reward for the head of bitter antislavery rival Samuel Walker "on or off his shoulders." But Walker and his men captured Titus at his farm. "As soon as we surrendered," wrote Titus, "several empty wagons which they brought with them were driven up and they commenced pillaging the premises; they took every movable article of any value…[and] even went so far as to take the clothing of my wife…They also told my servants that they were free and advised them to go to Topeka, yet they took the clothing that belonged to them." Titus begged Walker not to burn his home, to which Walker replied, "God damn you and God damn your house. Men, bring on the hay." It was torched and burned to the ground.

The proslavery armies struck back at the end of the month. David Atchison led about 1,500 Missourians into Kansas to "clean out" the area south of Lawrence. One of his columns split off to attack Osawatomie, the home of John Brown and his family. In the ensuing battle, one of Brown's sons was killed. Four other antislavery residents of the town also died. The Missourians lost two killed, but they leveled Osawatomie.

The new territorial governor, John W. Geary, finally managed to curtail the violence. He disbanded the existing state militia, organized a new militia and ordered all irregular troops out of the territory. He enlisted the help of the United States Army to keep the peace. Geary sent Federal troops to capture a free-soil band attacking the town of Hickory Point and, a few days later, headed off a band of Border Ruffians marching on Lawrence. Relative peace settled over Kansas.

Both sides exaggerated the violence in Kansas to promote their political agendas. Although proclaimed as "Bleeding Kansas," comparatively few men actually died. An 1859 federal inquiry concluded that more than 200 were killed in the fighting during 1855–56. Recent studies show that the actual number was 42 during those two years; in all, 56 men died in political killings between 1854 and 1861. Kansas was a violent place, but not

Proslavery partisans voting in territorial elections, from Albert Richardson, *Beyond the Mississippi,* *1857–1861. The State Historical Society of Missouri, Columbia.*

as violent as other places—California, for example, saw an estimated 538 killings during 1855 alone.

The territory's turmoil did not discourage migration, however. By the end of 1857, it was becoming clear that the antislavery forces were winning the population battle, if not the political battle, over whether Kansas would be a free or slave state. The territorial elections still produced a proslavery legislature, but by a smaller margin, and still tainted by widespread fraud. In the 1857 election, for example, an investigation proved that most of the proslavery votes came from "voters" whose names were copied from the Cincinnati city directory.

The years 1857 and 1858 saw a series of votes on constitutions to be submitted for statehood. Eventually, free-soilers and proslavery advocates submitted competing documents. Neither was approved, and the drive for statehood was stalemated for three years.

There was one last burst of atrocities in 1858. Antislavery bands of marauders in southeast Kansas were attacking their proslavery neighbors and crossing into Missouri to attack residents there. Charles Hamilton led some thirty-five proslavery men into Trading Post, Kansas, a small town in northeastern Linn County. He captured twenty men, "tried" them and found eleven guilty—presumably of supporting antislavery depredations. Hamilton took the eleven to a ravine on the Marais des Cygnes River, where they were lined up before a firing squad. Five died, four were wounded and two somehow escaped injury. Hamilton's men escaped without punishment.

Kansas voters finally ratified a fourth constitution—this one making Kansas a free state—in October 1859. Kansas was admitted into the Union on January 29, 1861—scarcely three months before the Civil War began.

Chapter 2

1861: The War Resumes

EARLY MOVES

Although a slave state, Missouri was not prepared to secede from the Union even if Abraham Lincoln won the presidential election of 1860. In the election, Lincoln won only 10 percent of the Missouri vote—mostly from St. Louis, where there was a substantial German immigrant population that was strongly antislavery. Democrat Stephen Douglas and Constitutional Unionist John C. Bell each received 35 percent of the vote; John C. Breckinridge (considered the proslavery candidate) received only 19 percent. Even in the Missouri River counties of Little Dixie, where most of Missouri's slaves and a number of wealthy slave owners lived, Bell did better than Breckinridge.

Missouri did, however, elect Claiborne Fox Jackson—a former Border Ruffian—as governor. Jackson favored secession and secretly took steps to bring Missouri into the Confederate States of America. Jackson coveted the United States Arsenal at St. Louis. The Arsenal held sixty thousand muskets, ninety thousand pounds of powder, 1.5 million ball cartridges, forty cannon and machinery to manufacture weapons. Much of the early military and political maneuvering in Missouri centered on gaining control of the Arsenal's weapons and ammunition.

Frank Blair Jr., a U.S. congressman and brother of Lincoln's postmaster general, sought to hold the Arsenal for the Union. He organized the Home Guards, mostly German American immigrants in St. Louis, to counter secessionist Minutemen. He also successfully sought to have Captain

Nathaniel Lyon, a staunch abolitionist, transferred to St. Louis to take command of the Arsenal.

In the meantime, Jackson sought and received from the legislature a call for a convention to consider secession on March 4. To Jackson's surprise and dismay, the convention voted overwhelmingly against secession. Missouri wanted to stay in the Union, to keep slavery and to avoid war. Nonetheless, war came on April 12, 1861. Governor Jackson condemned Lincoln's call for seventy-five thousand volunteers as "illegal, unconstitutional and revolutionary...inhuman and diabolical." Blair mustered his Home Guards into Federal service, and Lyon had those men available to him, in addition to the regulars stationed at the Arsenal.

Governor Jackson ordered the commander of the Missouri State Militia, Daniel Frost, to gather a force near St. Louis for "training." Frost assembled nine hundred men at Camp Jackson in Lindell's Grove (now the site of St. Louis University, then outside of the city).

The First Clash West of the Mississippi, Camp Jackson, St. Louis, Missouri, May 1861, from *Photographic History of the Civil War* (1911). Missouri State Guard troops at Camp Jackson near Lindell Grove were captured on May 10. While the prisoners were being marched through town, gunfire broke out. Federal troops fired into civilians, killing twenty-eight and wounding scores. *Library of Congress.*

1861: The War Resumes

Lyon suspected, with good reason, that Jackson and Frost intended to take the Arsenal. On May 10, with some 6,500 men, mostly German Americans from Blair's Home Guards, Lyon surrounded Camp Jackson and demanded its surrender. Frost, knowing he could not defend against such an overwhelming force, gave up without a fight. But while Lyon's troops were marching the prisoners to town, someone in the crowd of civilians watching the procession fired at the German troops. The Federals returned the fire. Before the mêlée was over, 28 persons were killed. Lyon took the prisoners to the Arsenal, where they were paroled.

Jackson reacted swiftly to the affair. The legislature authorized him to activate the Missouri State Guard and placed the state on a war footing. Sterling Price, a Mexican War veteran, was put in charge of the four thousand men who gathered at Jefferson City. Although no overt combat had broken out between the state troops under Price and the Federal troops under Lyon, the prospects of a peaceful resolution were not good. In an attempt to defuse the situation, Lyon's superior in St. Louis, General William Harney, reached an agreement with Price that he would not send Federal troops outside the city if Price "kept the peace" elsewhere in the state. Blair condemned the arrangement as naïve and got Lincoln's consent to replace Harney with Lyon.

On June 11, Jackson and Price met with Lyon at the Planter's House Hotel in St. Louis to try to come to an accommodation. Lyon, incensed, refused any deal along the lines of that agreed to by Harney that would restrict Federal troop movements with the state. "[R]ather than concede to the State of Missouri the right to dictate to my government in any matter, however unimportant," Lyon declared, "I would rather see you... and every man, woman, and child in the state, dead and buried. This means war!"

Jackson and Price ordered the bridges between Jefferson City and St. Louis burned. The remainder of the Missouri State Guard reported to Boonville and Lexington, upriver from the capital. On June 13, Lyon boarded 1,700 troops on steamers and sailed up the Missouri River. He easily defeated a small force near Boonville, but the bulk of the Missouri troops escaped. Jackson and Price worked their way to southwest Missouri. On July 5, Federal troops under Franz Sigel, a prominent German American politician, intercepted them north of Carthage. In a running battle, Sigel retreated through the town and finally managed to elude the larger force. Price's Missouri State Guard joined with Confederate forces under Ben McCulloch at Wilson's Creek, about ten miles southwest of Springfield.

The Fateful Meeting at the St. Louis Hotel, from John McElroy, *The Struggle for Missouri* (National Tribune Company, 1909). On June 11, 1861, at the Planter's House, Union general Nathaniel Lyon (left) confronted Governor Claiborne Fox Jackson and Missouri State Guard commander General Sterling Price. Lyon declared, "This means war!" and gave Jackson and Price one hour to leave the city. *The State Historical Society of Missouri, Columbia.*

1861: The War Resumes

Lyon arrived in Springfield on July 13, but his and Sigel's men together totaled only about nine thousand men—far fewer than the Confederate army only a short distance away. Nevertheless, Lyon was nothing if not bold, and he decided to make a surprise attack on the enemy. On the night of August 9, Lyon led one column to Wilson's Creek, and Sigel led another to take the Confederates from the rear. The plan nearly succeeded the next morning. But Sigel's men mistook a Louisiana regiment from McCulloch's army for an Iowa regiment that wore similar uniforms. Sigel's men were routed. The Confederates turned their entire force against Lyon. Lyon was killed leading a charge of Kansas troops, and the surviving Union officers realized that retreat was their only option. And retreat they did—eventually, all the way to Rolla, the railhead of the southwestern branch of the Pacific Railroad and Union supply base.

Price decided to move north again. On the way, he brushed aside a desultory attack by Kansas cavalry under Jim Lane (now a general) at Drywood Creek in the Battle of the Mules—so called because the fight began when Price's men captured eighty-six mules. The Kansans retreated to their base at Fort Scott, Kansas, just across the state line, in some panic because they thought Price was now going to invade the state.

Price instead continued his march northward to the secessionist stronghold of Lexington, on the Missouri River. The town was held by 3,500 Union soldiers under Colonel James A. Mulligan. Two thousand troops from northeast Missouri—a force that once included (for about two weeks) a man named Samuel Clemens—joined Price in the siege. Price's men drove off a relief force sent from Mexico, Missouri. Despite Mulligan's pleas for help to the department's new commander, General John C. Frémont (the "Pathfinder" and former Republican presidential candidate), no other help came. Price's men soaked bales of hemp and used them as mobile breastworks in attacking the Federal lines. After seven days, the Union forces at Lexington surrendered. This engagement, known as the Battle of the Hemp Bales, was the last large clash between the armies in Missouri for two years. There were no more colorful names for battles, either, as the war became increasingly vicious.

After taking Lexington, Price learned that Frémont was at last moving against him. Fearful of being cut off, Price retreated once again to southern Missouri. Although he tried to get McCulloch and other Confederate commanders to join in attacks against the Federals, they all refused. Formal military operations stalled.

In November, what was left of the Missouri legislature passed an ordinance of secession. But Missouri's functioning civil government was firmly in the hands of the Union. Hamilton R. Gamble, who had skillfully led the anti-secession forces in the March convention, was selected as "provisional" governor. The members of the convention acted as a legislature until the next election.

The presence of a large Confederate army in the state contributed to keeping guerrilla attacks to a minimum, especially compared to the levels such fighting would reach later. There were no large guerrilla bands that roamed the countryside and hid out in the brush. But Union commanders were concerned, nevertheless, with sporadic actions where men would appear to burn railroad bridges, tear up the tracks or fire into passing trains and then return to their farms.

Hamilton R. Gamble. Gamble was a leader of the Missouri Conservatives. He was named provisional governor of the state in 1861 when the regular legislature was suspended. *The State Historical Society of Missouri, Columbia.*

And, indeed, such acts of sabotage could take a terrible toll. At about 5:00 p.m. on September 3, twelve to fourteen men burned down the Hannibal & St. Joseph Railroad's bridge across the Platte River, between St. Joseph and Easton. At 11:00 p.m., a westbound train plunged into the river, killing thirteen persons and injuring seventy-five others. The culprits were not caught, to the frustration of Federal commanders.

JENNISON'S RAID

The most serious depredations in Missouri came not from Confederate guerrillas but from Jayhawkers bent on revenge and loot. Among the most notorious was Charles "Doc" Jennison. Jennison, a short man with an affinity for unusual outfits, had experience in attacking civilians and raiding Missouri during the Bleeding Kansas days.

A few days after being driven back to Fort Scott, Lane ordered Jennison ostensibly to pursue Price as he made his way northward. Jennison never

1861: The War Resumes

Jemison's [sic] *Jayhawkers*, a drawing by Adalbert John Volck, *V. Blada's War Sketches* (1864). Although it misspelled his name, this drawing depicts a typical raid by Doc Jennison's Kansas raiders, also known as Red Legs for the distinctive red leather gaiters they wore. *Library of Congress.*

caught up with Price, but he did not return empty-handed: he brought back two hundred head of cattle and a number of slaves, or "contraband," as they were then called.

Later in September, Lane himself led a "smart little army" of 1,500, which proceeded to loot the Missouri counties just across the border. On September 23, Lane's men clashed briefly with Confederates in Osceola, the county seat of St. Clair County. After driving off the enemy, the Jayhawkers proceeded to rob the bank, pillage stores and homes and bombard the courthouse with a cannon. Nine men were given a quick trial and executed. Lane's Jayhawkers drank their fill of whiskey and stole 350 horses, 400 head of cattle, flour and other supplies. Lane himself claimed a piano and a number of silk dresses. The Kansans were so drunk that many had to ride home in wagons.

Kansas governor Charles Robinson commissioned Jennison a colonel and authorized him to raise a regiment of cavalry. This unit, officially the Seventh Kansas Cavalry but known as the Independent Mounted Kansas Jayhawkers, raided Missouri in November 1861. It was led in the field by Daniel B. Anthony, a leader of the early abolitionist settlers, a Leavenworth newspaperman and now commissioned a lieutenant colonel. Although Jennison was its titular head, Anthony was "very careful not to permit him to write or do anything unless done under the supervision of some of his friends who have good judgment." The Seventh Kansas counted among its members John Brown's son, John Brown Jr., and a company led by ex-convict Marshall Cleveland that was composed "mostly of criminals and ruffians."

The unit's first foray was into Jackson and Cass Counties; its mission was to protect Union wagon trains and to put down the rebellion in the area. Instead, the regiment principally engaged in burning homes and crops, while chasing the residents into the fields. After giving the citizens of Independence "a little touch of the misfortunes of war," they marched back to Kansas City burdened with plunder and accompanied by many slaves—some of whom they armed as soldiers.

Later in the month, the Seventh Kansas once again went on a rampage. On the way to West Point, Missouri, in northeastern Bates County, the cavalry burned the houses in its path, leaving columns of smoke to mark its progress. Anthony's men stole 150 mules and 40 horses and freed 129 Negroes, to whom he gave some of the livestock and household goods taken along the way.

On New Year's Day 1862, the Kansans attacked Dayton, Missouri, burning more than forty homes to the ground. The village of Columbus suffered a similar fate the following week. Anthony led them to Pleasant Hill, where the regiment stole $10,000 worth of livestock, prompting one resident to remark, "The country is being ruined." The raiders also destroyed Morristown and Kingsville. No distinction was made between Union and Southern sympathizers—if you lived in Missouri, that was enough to justify burning your home and taking your horses, cows and mules. The result was that many men who were at least neutral decided to join the Confederate army or to form guerrilla bands.

Although many Kansans applauded the raids, in mid-January, Major General Henry Halleck, by now the department commander, finally ordered that Jennison's regiment and other Kansans not be allowed to enter Missouri except with his express approval. In his opinion, such raids were not going to discourage the rebellion. Lane's and Jennison's men were "no better than a band of robbers; they cross the line, rob, steal, plunder, and burn whatever they can lay their hands upon. They disgrace the name and uniform of American soldiers...A few more such raids...will make [Missouri] as unanimous against us as is Eastern Virginia."

Chapter 3

1862: Guerrillas Fill the Void

D espite his success at Wilson's Creek and Lexington, General Sterling Price could not hold Missouri. In an unusual winter campaign, General Samuel Curtis drove Price's army from Springfield into northern Arkansas. Price joined with Confederate troops commanded by General Earl Van Dorn. They attempted to cut off Curtis but failed. Curtis defeated the Confederates at Pea Ridge on March 6–8, 1862.

This battle effectively ended Price's effort to retake Missouri for the South for two years. He left the Missouri State Guard to become a Confederate general. Many of the Missourians, however, did not follow him. They chose to return home. And many of the returnees became guerrillas.

THE LIEBER CODE

"Old Brains"—Major General Henry W. Halleck—was meticulous, hardworking and very bright: the model of the quintessential military bureaucrat. At the age of forty-six, he was "in perfect health, and full of vigor. As he peered at us out of his large black eyes underneath heavy dark eyebrows, and a high massive forehead, he looked wondrous wise." He made "rogues tremble and even honest men look about them to be sure they have not been up to some mischief."

Halleck was not only a West Point graduate but also a lawyer and the author of books on military theory, land titles and international law. In his spare time during the war, he worked on a four-volume translation from the French of Jomini's *Life of Napoleon*.

Like almost every professional soldier, he had little respect for the unconventional warfare waged by guerrillas. Halleck believed that war, although brutal, should be waged honorably, according to accepted principles. Soldiers did not murder one another. Rather, they fought under legal orders on fields of honor. If captured, they could be paroled—allowed to go free on their promise not to take up arms again until properly exchanged. Soldiers did not shoot civilians or prisoners. Soldiers took from civilians only what they needed and even then gave a receipt that could be redeemed later for reparations from the government. While there was, of course, a place in military affairs for cavalry raids behind lines that could disrupt an enemy's communications and supplies, the raiders were or should be under the command of officers commissioned by the government and acting under proper military orders.

General Sterling Price. Price was a former Missouri governor and the commander of the Missouri State Guard at the Battles of Wilson's Creek, Lexington and Pea Ridge. In 1864, he led an invasion of Missouri that ended in defeat at the Battle of Westport, near Kansas City. Price reluctantly accepted the guerrillas' assistance in harassing Federal supply lines. *Library of Congress*.

Guerrillas did not fit this idealized description. During the short time he directly oversaw operations in Missouri, Halleck became frustrated with the hit-and-run nature of guerrilla warfare. He was particularly concerned with the burning of railroad bridges because (as seen in the Platte River disaster) the consequences could be so devastating to life and property. "This is not usually done by armed and open enemies," Halleck wrote, "but by pretended quiet citizens, living on their farms. A bridge or building is set on fire, and the culprit an hour after is quietly plowing or working in his field. The civil courts can give us no assistance, as they are very generally unreliable. There is no alternative but to enforce martial law. Our army here is almost as much in hostile country as it was in Mexico."

General Henry Halleck. "Old Brains" was a lawyer, author and military scholar. He was commander of the Department of Missouri from November 1861 to March 1862. Halleck was later appointed the commander of all the Union armies, an administrative post that suited his talents. *Library of Congress.*

Napoleon contended with guerrillas in Spain, where his solution was immediate death when caught. Halleck proclaimed a similar policy: every man who becomes a guerrilla "forfeits his life and becomes an outlaw." He warned that "if they join any guerrilla band they will not, if captured, be treated as ordinary prisoners of war, but will be hung as robbers and murderers."

Some guerrillas became enraged when they found out about this order and vowed to pursue a similar course—no quarter for anyone captured. General Price objected to Halleck's order, protesting against the execution of persons acting under his orders to destroy railroads and bridges because such activities were "recognized by the civilized world...as distinctly lawful and proper." Halleck wrote back that if such raiders were in uniform and duly organized as soldiers of the Confederacy, then they would be treated as prisoners of war if captured. But if they acted under the pretense of being peaceful citizens, they would not be entitled to such treatment.

Whether General Halleck's order began the cycle of retaliation is debatable. More likely, it simply recognized existing practice.

Guerrillas were inherently informal groupings. There was no command structure. The commanders led by force of personality. And if guerrillas decided to shoot a prisoner or a civilian, there was no disciplinary system in place, such as courts-martial, to punish the offenders—even if the guerrilla leader thought they deserved it. Moreover, guerrillas, of course, had no prisons or other facilities to which to send captives. Although some presumed to parole their prisoners, virtually none of the Missouri guerrillas held any office in the Confederate army that formally gave them the power to do so. They had two alternatives: either let the prisoners go or kill them. The guerrillas frequently chose the latter course.

Federal troops, on the other hand, could send their prisoners to St. Louis or elsewhere for trial and imprisonment or execution. As a practical matter, though, the enforcement of Halleck's order (and similar directives issued later in the war) fell to the junior officers and enlisted men in the field. Many of the units, especially early in the war, were little better than what Halleck called "military rabble." They lacked training and discipline. Many were themselves looking for revenge, either for prewar controversies or for depredations committed against their own families or homes.

Moreover, the nature of guerrilla warfare—where "battles" most often began as ambushes—made Federal troop movements in any but the largest numbers subject to surprise attacks. Small patrols, wagon trains, railroad trains, steamboats, stagecoaches—all could be the victim of a guerrilla attack at any time. Venturing outside the military posts in guerrilla country put soldiers under tremendous psychological stress.

After taking command of the entire army, General Halleck, being the careful scholar, sought the assistance of another scholar to develop a more formal, army-wide policy for dealing with guerrillas. On August 6, 1862, he wrote to Professor Francis W. Lieber to ask him to develop a codification of the rules of war, in particular those relating to guerrillas. Lieber, a veteran of the Napoleonic Wars, had been a professor at the University of Jena before fleeing Prussian rule. He immigrated to the United States. Before the Civil War, he taught at South Carolina College. In 1862, he was teaching at New York's Columbia College. Lieber had sons in both the Union and Confederate armies. The latter was killed while on active service.

Professor Francis Lieber. At Halleck's request, Professor Lieber wrote the Lieber Code, a version of which Halleck issued as a guide to Union troops for the conduct of the guerrilla war that sanctioned their execution as robbers and pirates. *Library of Congress.*

Lieber classified the bands fighting behind the lines into two categories. "Partisans" were soldiers authorized by the government and serving under military orders and control. They should be treated as ordinary soldiers. If captured, they were entitled to the privileges of prisoners of war. They could be executed only if, after a trial, there was proof that they had committed a capital offense.

"Guerrillas," on the other hand, were persons "who resort to occasional fighting and occasional assuming of peaceful habits." They were not subject to military control and engaged in destruction for destruction's sake, with no specific military or strategic purpose. Lieber regarded guerrillas as brigands who must resort to murder because they had no practical way to hold prisoners of war. Their leaders could impose only the loosest discipline, if that. Lieber recommended that captured guerrillas be executed—unless the government decided for other reasons to be more lenient.

This document, known as the Lieber Code, became the basis for General Halleck's General Order No. 100, issued April 24, 1863, that provided a legal framework for the war. It introduced the concept of military necessity, by which soldiers could confiscate or destroy private property when needed to defeat the enemy. And it directed that guerrillas, when captured, were "not entitled to the privileges of prisoners of war, but shall be treated summarily as highway robbers or pirates." Likewise, civilians who assisted the enemy were subject to execution. Thus, the Lieber Code affirmed Halleck's earlier orders and explicitly made legal the hanging or shooting of captured guerrillas.

Confederate authorities, while protesting the Union's harsh treatment of guerrillas, were ambivalent toward their activities. Although imbued with the same tradition of "noble" warfare, they used or at least tolerated guerrilla warfare for whatever military advantage it could bring. In 1862, the Confederate Congress passed the Partisan Ranger Act, giving legal sanction to guerrilla bands. The statute was primarily directed at what Lieber would call "partisans," such as Mosby's Rangers in Virginia. It required partisans to operate under the same regulations as the regular army.

The Partisan Ranger Act had little effect in Missouri, where guerrillas were more or less spontaneous gatherings of men from a particular locality who got together for various reasons—ideology, revenge, protection—to carry the war to Union soldiers and civilian sympathizers. General Thomas Hindman, the Confederate commander of the Trans-Mississippi Department, which included Missouri, issued Order No. 17 authorizing the enrollment of independent guerrillas into his army (similar to the Partisan Ranger Act).

Hindman called on persons who were not in the army to "organize themselves into independent companies of mounted men or infantry." They were to "commence operations...without waiting for special instructions." Their duty was "to cut off Federal pickets, scouts, foraging parties, and trains, and to kill pilots and others on gunboats and transports, attacking them day and night, and using the greatest vigor in their movements." The guerrillas were to be governed by the same regulations as other troops, and the commanders were to be held responsible for the men's "good conduct and efficiency" and to report to him "from time to time."

No guerrillas ever complied with this order, and Hindman himself quickly came to rue its issuance. By the end of 1862, he was disgusted that the guerrillas who were supposed to be part of his command operating behind enemy lines were committing many depredations against citizens, no matter which side they supported, "doing no good, but much harm, in every way." Although some Missouri guerrillas were commissioned officers of the Confederate army, most were not. Those who were officers were somewhat more likely to release captured Union soldiers on parole, at least early in the war. Otherwise, it made little difference in how they operated.

MILITARY COMMISSIONS: "TRIBUNALS OF NECESSITY"

Murder and destruction of property were, of course, crimes under the laws of Missouri. But in many parts of the state, the courts were either inoperative or controlled by known secessionists. General Frémont had declared martial law in the state in 1861. But that did not alone solve the problem.

Therefore, General Halleck—as befit the prudent lawyer he was—looked to precedent for a solution. During the Mexican War, General Winfield Scott established military commissions to try civil and criminal matters between American soldiers and Mexican citizens. The Mexican courts were also not functioning or hostile to the invading army. And so Halleck turned to military commissions in Missouri.

Despite being established under military authority for the express purpose of trying not only suspected guerrillas but also civilians suspected of aiding them, the military commissions provided a measure of due process. The rules of evidence and procedure used in courts-martial applied. The defendants were entitled to know the charges against them, to representation, to confront their accusers and to present evidence of innocence or in mitigation. Halleck would not allow commissions to try anyone for treason because that was a crime defined in the Constitution and left to the federal civil court system. The department commander reviewed all decisions, frequently reduced the punishment and occasionally overturned the conviction altogether. President Lincoln insisted that no one convicted by the commissions be executed without his specific review and approval.

Trial before a military commission was therefore not a foregone conclusion. For example, Jefferson T. Jones, a prominent secessionist from Callaway County, was acquitted of assisting the enemy despite testimony from captured guerrillas that he allowed them to eat and spend the night at his home, and that he kept suspiciously large amounts of gunpowder and shot at his plantation.

Guerrillas who had been taken prisoner frequently claimed, with some justification, that they were forced to join the bushwhackers or that, while they were members of a particular band, they did not participate in the killings with which they were charged. These men could at least avoid the death penalty, if not imprisonment.

QUANTRILL EMERGES

Price's retreat from Missouri left the state—particularly its western region—vulnerable to Union raiders such as Jennison and Lane. Returning soldiers from the Missouri State Guard and local civilians began to organize informal groups to protect their homes and families and to retaliate against Jayhawker depredations. The most celebrated of these guerrilla bands was led by William C. Quantrill. Even today, anyone with the slightest knowledge of Civil War guerrillas knows of Quantrill.

Quantrill had been a member of Price's army, fighting at Wilson's Creek and Lexington. He returned to Jackson County when Price's army went to Arkansas. He joined a group pursuing some of Jennison's men in December 1861. By Christmas, he had organized his own band of guerrillas. They clashed with the Jayhawkers in early 1862. By March, he was already well known enough to be reported by one Federal officer as the "notorious Quantrill and his gang of robbers."

Quantrill entered the public consciousness as an even more "notorious" guerrilla with a raid on Aubrey, Kansas, just across the state line from Cass County (southwest of Kansas City). Following a pattern that would become familiar, Quantrill led forty men into town at daybreak. They shot three civilians, set fire to one house, took a Union soldier as hostage (and released him a few days later) and left as quickly as they arrived.

March 1862 saw a number of clashes between Federal troops and guerrillas, some led by Quantrill and some led by others. On March 22, Quantrill's men captured a Union sergeant detailed to guard a bridge across the Little Blue River in southwest Jackson County. By then, Quantrill had learned of General Halleck's "no quarter" policy. He shot the sergeant himself, and his men burned the bridge. The attack prompted a search by Federal troops for the perpetrators. They trailed Quantrill to the house of David Tate. That night, the Federal cavalry caught Quantrill and about twenty men inside the house. After refusing Union demands to surrender, the guerrillas began a terrific gun battle. The cavalry set the house on fire to drive the Rebels out. Quantrill and his men escaped by knocking down a burning wall and running for the woods. They left seven dead and three prisoners behind.

1862: Guerrillas Fill the Void

Quantrill and Raiders Headed for Lawrence, from R.P. Bradley, *Outlaws of the Border: A Complete and Authentic History of the Lives of Frank and Jesse James* (1882). The Lawrence raid was the most notorious but by no means the only guerrilla attack that Quantrill led into Kansas. *The State Historical Society of Missouri, Columbia.*

Other guerrillas were active in western Missouri at the same time. Ben Parker led a group that attacked the steamboat *Rowena* near Sibley, in eastern Jackson County. A few days later, he led forty men on a raid across the Missouri River on the town of Liberty, in Clay County. Two weeks later, Federal cavalry captured Parker and dispersed his men in western Johnson County. Parker's men laid low for several months and joined Quantrill in the fall.

At the end of March, Federal troops once again surprised Quantrill in camp, this time in eastern Jackson County. After a ninety-minute firefight, the guerrillas once more escaped into the woods. Another unit caught Quantrill's men the next day, but after a very brief gunfight, Quantrill's men broke off the action and melted into the brush. The Federals continued their pursuit of Quantrill, and on April 16, they trapped him for the third time in Jackson County, and for the third time he evaded capture.

The Union commander, General James Totten, issued an order reciting the depredations committed by the guerrillas, blaming them all on "a well-known and desperate leader of these outlaws by the name of Quantrill." He directed that "[a]ll those found in arms and opposition to the laws and legitimate authorities, who are familiarly known as guerrillas, jayhawkers, murderers, marauders, and horse-thieves, will be shot down by the military upon the spot when found perpetrating their foul acts."

Totten's threats did not deter Quantrill or other guerrillas in western Missouri. On May 16, Quantrill's men attacked a Union patrol from the First Missouri Cavalry acting as an escort for the mail. The Rebels lay in wait at a cut on the road from Harrisonville to Independence where it crossed the Little Blue River. When the cavalry entered the cut, the guerrillas sprang the ambush, gunning down virtually all of the soldiers with pistol fire in the confined space. Two died, nine were wounded and only two escaped unharmed.

After this attack, Quantrill's men hid for about a month for lack of ammunition. He and his trusted lieutenant, George Todd, traveled to Hannibal to buy percussion caps for their weapons. On June 11, Quantrill's men were back in action. Over the space of eleven days, his men ambushed another mail escort, attacked and robbed a stagecoach, clashed with a Union cavalry patrol and attacked another steamboat—all in Jackson County.

In early July, a patrol of the First Iowa Cavalry came upon Quantrill's camp in Cass County. They chased the guerrillas for the next two days. Finally, on July 11, Quantrill turned on them. Six miles west of Pleasant Hill, he set an ambush for his pursuers at Big Creek. As the Federal column caught up with the Rebels, a group of Quantrill's men milled about in a clearing, pretending surprise. Lured on by this act, the cavalry charged into the clearing, where it was met by a fusillade of bullets. The cavalry fell back but quickly recovered and began firing their carbines at the guerrillas. The guerrillas retreated into nearby wooded ravines. For the next three hours, the two sides exchanged gunfire at close range in the dense woods. Federal reinforcements arrived, and the battle continued with renewed ferocity. At last, the guerrillas dispersed and escaped. The cavalry lost ten killed and nineteen wounded. Quantrill's losses are not known but were probably about the same.

Quantrill's next major battle resulted in his official commissioning as a Confederate officer. In the summer of 1862, Confederate colonels Upton Hay, John Hughes and Gideon Thompson were recruiting men in western Missouri to serve in the Confederate army. They joined Quantrill in a camp just west of Independence. Together, the Confederate force numbered some 600 men, plus Quantrill's approximately 150. Independence was held by a Union force of 300 men.

Early on the morning of August 11, Quantrill and his men rode into the Independence town square, taking the Federals completely by surprise and trapping their commander in his bedclothes on the second floor of his headquarters. In the meantime, the three Confederate colonels led their recruits against the main Union camp on the edge of town. The fight continued for about four hours until the Federals finally surrendered. They lost 37 men killed, 63 wounded and 150 captured. The rest fled to Kansas City. Colonel Hughes was killed in the attack.

The next day, Colonel Thompson swore Quantrill in as a captain in the Confederate army, but whether under the Partisan Ranger Act or General Hindman's Order No. 17 is not clear.

Stung by the humiliation at Independence, Union commanders sent several columns to converge on Jackson County to catch those responsible for the defeat. Confederate troops defeated one of those columns at the Battle of Lone Jack, in southeastern Jackson County. Quantrill himself was not at Lone Jack, but some of his men were. His band did, however, continue to operate in Jackson County, venturing out from their hideout in the woods and ravines of the eastern part of the county to clash with Federal troops in late August.

On September 6, Quantrill again took the war to Kansas, this time raiding Olathe. They surprised and captured 125 recruits from the Twelfth Kansas Infantry, killed 3 civilians, looted the town and destroyed the local newspaper. Quantrill bragged to former acquaintances about his captaincy in the Confederate army. The raid did not go unpunished. The Sixth Kansas Cavalry from Fort Leavenworth tracked Quantrill's men into Cass County and overtook them on the Grand River. There followed an eleven-day pursuit through Cass, Jackson, Johnson and Lafayette Counties that ended only when the guerrillas disbanded and dispersed. The Kansas troops recaptured most of the booty taken from Olathe and used the occasion to burn houses and take slaves back to Leavenworth. They killed only two guerrillas and lost one man themselves.

By early October, Quantrill reunited his band. On October 6, they ambushed a column of the Fifth Missouri Cavalry near Sibley, a river town northeast of Kansas City. On the evening of October 17, Quantrill captured a Federal wagon train near Shawneetown, Kansas, southwest of Kansas City, killing about half its military escort. The next day, they rode into the town itself, killing ten men and looting the town—primarily for clothes—and then burned it to the ground.

In early November, Quantrill was ready to move south for the winter. The leaves were off the trees, and it was more difficult to hide from Federal patrols in the woods of Jackson County. On their way, the guerrillas came upon a wagon train near Harrisonville, Cass County. They killed ten soldiers and teamsters and took five others captive, including the commander. A

Federal patrol from the same outfit chased the guerrillas, overtaking them at 9:00 that night. The Union cavalry killed six of Quantrill's men before he could escape.

Quantrill's guerrillas had one more skirmish before leaving the state for the winter. He met a group of three hundred recruits led by Colonel Warner Lewis near Lamar, Missouri, in Barton County. They decided to attack a detachment of the Eighth Missouri Cavalry stationed in the town. Quantrill's men fell upon the Federals at 10:00 p.m. and drove them into the brick county courthouse. The courthouse was nearly impregnable. When Colonel Lewis's men failed to show up for the assault, Quantrill broke off the attack. The guerrillas lost about five men killed and several wounded. The Union troops' loss was three killed and three mortally wounded.

Quantrill's men joined General Hindman in Arkansas. Like other Confederate generals, Hindman was ambivalent about the use of guerrillas. He praised Quantrill's activities, writing that they "rendered important services, destroying wagon trains and transports, tearing up railways, breaking telegraph lines, capturing towns, and thus compelling the enemy to keep there a large force that might have been employed elsewhere." But their refusal to follow orders and indiscriminate violence also offended his sense of military propriety.

During the winter of 1862–63, Quantrill traveled to Richmond to seek a commission from President Davis as a colonel and to raise a partisan ranger brigade in Missouri. In his absence, Hindman assigned his men, commanded for the time being by William Gregg, to Jo Shelby's cavalry brigade. They fought with distinction in the Battles of Cane Hill and Prairie Grove in December 1862. This was their only service in the regular army. Quantrill's men would be ready the next spring to return to western Missouri to resume guerrilla activities.

JOSEPH C. PORTER, RECRUITING BEHIND THE LINES AND THE PALMYRA MASSACRE

In contrast to the informal and haphazard recruitment of civilian guerrillas, such as Quantrill's band, the Confederacy also sponsored the enrollment of men into the regular army from behind Union lines in Missouri. Although these men were supposed to join the Confederate army in Arkansas and served under commissioned officers, they frequently attacked towns, robbed and killed civilians and ambushed Federal troops in a manner indistinguishable from guerrillas who lacked any such official trappings. Much of the guerrilla warfare during the spring and summer of 1862 in northeast Missouri was between these recruiting bands and Federal troops.

One of the best-known recruiters was Joseph Porter. Before the war, he lived in Lewis County, in northeastern Missouri. Porter served under Price at Lexington and Pea Ridge, rising in rank from a private to lieutenant colonel. His plan was to return to his home to gather recruits for the army—he was sure there were hundreds who were waiting to join. He also would, when conditions were favorable, carry out attacks on Federal soldiers to "stimulate enlistments...The greater activity I display, the more Federals I shall keep from the front." His recruiting trip lasted for several months during the summer of 1862 and provoked an international controversy over the treatment of Rebel guerrillas.

Porter returned to Lewis County, and by June 17, forty-three men had joined his band. They captured four Federal soldiers in Marion County and paroled them. They moved south to carry out sporadic attacks in Lewis County. From there, Porter took his men north to the Iowa border. Federal cavalry caught up with him at Cherry Grove and, during a running battle that lasted a good part of the day, killed twelve and wounded twenty of his men. While Porter was in Schuyler County, his brother Jim surprised a company of Federal cavalry near Newark, in Knox County. The cavalrymen took refuge in a brick house, where they held off the guerrillas. In the meantime, Jim Porter's men sacked the town. Another company from Porter's command, led by Raphael Smith, raided towns in Lewis County and murdered at least one civilian.

Porter clashed with Federal troops three more times in mid-July. On July 13, he led 250 men into Memphis, Missouri, and captured it with little trouble. The rebels took eighty-two muskets from the armory and a quantity of Union blue uniforms. They herded all the men of military age into the courthouse and then (according to Union newspapers) proceeded to steal what they wanted from the town's stores. Before leaving town, some of Porter's men hanged Dr. William Aylward, a prominent Union sympathizer.

On July 18, Porter was still in Scotland County, southwest of Memphis. He was being trailed by cavalry from Merrill's Horse (Second Missouri Cavalry) and the Eleventh Cavalry Missouri State Militia (MSM) under Major John Y. Clopper. Porter set a trap for them on the Middle Fabius River, at a place known to the locals as Vassar Hill. He left a few men on the bridge to pretend that they were tearing it up. When the Federals appeared, the men fled. Porter had stationed the bulk of his force a short distance up the road. The unsuspecting cavalry charged into the ambush, where many were gunned down by musket and shotgun fire. Porter withdrew to another, even better position. Once again, the Union cavalry charged up the road, and once again they were met with a devastating hail of gunfire. In all, Clopper's men charged and were repulsed six times. By the time Porter left the area for good, Clopper had suffered twenty-four killed and fifty-nine wounded.

Porter marched south to Florida, Missouri, where on July 22 he encountered about fifty men from the Third Iowa Cavalry. In a brief firefight, the Iowans killed two of Porter's men and themselves suffered about thirty wounded. According to Joseph Mudd, one of Porter's men and a postwar chronicler of the expedition, several female residents (including the local schoolteacher) ran out of the houses during the battle to encourage the Rebels in their attack.

After the Florida skirmish, Porter continued south to a camp on Auxvasse Creek, in northeastern Callaway County. On July 25, he was joined by 75 men from the guerrilla band led by Alvin Cobb of nearby Montgomery County and group of 65 recruits from Boone County. While accounts vary, Porter likely had about 350 men under his command.

The Union authorities were keeping track of Porter. On July 27, General John M. Schofield ordered Colonel Odon Guitar, a prominent Columbia lawyer before the war, to take two companies of his Ninth Cavalry MSM from Jefferson City and to join Lieutenant Colonel Shaffer's detachment of Merrill's Horse. Guitar crossed the Missouri River and arrived at Fulton in central Callaway County. He added a company of the Third Iowa Cavalry stationed there and marched along the Fulton-Mexico road toward Porter's reported location at Brown's Spring, eleven miles north.

General Odon Guitar. Guitar was a Columbia, Missouri lawyer. He raised and commanded the Ninth Cavalry, Missouri State Militia, one of the most effective guerrilla-hunting units in the Union army. *From the Joan Wyant Collection, The State Historical Society of Missouri, Columbia.*

1862: Guerrillas Fill the Void

Guitar found the Brown's Spring camp empty. Porter had decided to move to a better position, where he awaited the advance of the Union force. He deliberately left a well-marked trail along Auxvasse Creek in the hope that the Federals would fall into another ambush, as they had at Vassar Hill. The next day, July 28, Porter's men waited in the underbrush at Moore's Mill (near present-day Calwood) for the enemy to advance. Guitar, in the meantime, met Shaffer's force. He directed Shaffer to move along the east side of Auxvasse Creek while he led his men along the west side.

About 1:00 p.m., Porter sprang the trap. His men fired two volleys into Guitar's advance, stopping them in their tracks. The remainder of Guitar's force came up, dismounted and deployed on either side of the road in the brush. There were no attempts at a heroic mounted charge as at Vassar Hill. Guitar had two artillery pieces manned by the Third Indiana Battery. He ordered one of the guns forward to the center of his position, where it opened fire with shell and canister on the Rebels. The second gun unlimbered and directed its fire at some of Porter's men who were apparently trying to get around Guitar's left flank.

The firefight continued for an hour. It was a typical hot July day. Porter's men had taken up their positions before finishing their breakfast, and there was little water available. Finally, Porter called out: "Boys, we can't stand this; we shall have to charge them. Forward! Charge!" Guitar described what happened next:

> *Just at this moment a heavy fire was opened on our left followed by the wildest yells, and in quick succession came a storm of leaden hail upon our center and a rush for our guns. On they came tearing through the brush. Their fire had proved most destructive, killing and wounding four of the cannoneers and quite a number in the immediate vicinity of the guns… Now was the crisis; the buckshot rattled upon the leaves like the pattering of hail…Our men, who had reserved their fire until now, springing to their feet, poured a well directed volley into their ranks and the remaining cannoneer delivered them a charge of canister which had been left in his gun since the fall of his comrades.*

The Rebels briefly seized the cannon. At that point, Shaffer's men arrived. Guitar deployed one company on his right and the rest on his left. Porter fell back to a line about twenty to fifty yards in advance of his original position. The fight continued for another three hours in blazing heat. The Rebels realized that they were running out of ammunition.

Porter, after making sure his supplies were secure, ordered a retreat. The Confederates withdrew from the field.

Both sides were exhausted, hungry and thirsty. They had battled each other in extreme heat in dense woods so thick it was difficult to see thirty feet in normal circumstances, let alone with clouds of smoke from muskets hanging in the air. Porter's men were too weary to continue the fight, and Guitar's men were too weary to pursue them.

The Battle of Moore's Mill resulted in Union losses of 20 dead and 55 wounded and in Confederate losses of 60 dead and 120 wounded. Guitar became a Union hero and was later promoted to brigadier general. In this battle and later actions, he and his men of the Ninth Missouri Cavalry earned a well-deserved reputation as guerrilla hunters.

Throughout the war, Union headquarters demanded the Missouri commanders supply troops for the armies fighting elsewhere, leaving few

Ninth Cavalry, Missouri State Militia. The men of the MSM were generally well trained and well equipped. They did not have to serve outside Missouri. Their mission was to hunt guerrillas, allowing other Federal units to be sent to General Grant for the Vicksburg Campaign and to General Sherman for the Atlanta Campaign. *The State Historical Society of Missouri, Columbia.*

regular Federal forces to deal with the guerrillas. On July 22, 1862, General Schofield sought to solve his manpower problem by issuing General Order No. 19. This directive required all able-bodied men between the ages of nineteen and forty-five to report within six days to sign up for the Enrolled Missouri Militia (EMM). Members of the EMM were to remain at home until needed, at which time they were to report to a specified rallying point. Over fifty-two thousand men signed up and were organized into seventy regiments. These outfits were generally ill equipped and poorly supplied. The state was supposed to pay them because the EMM was not considered Federal service. The men brought their own weapons. Because the government did not give them uniforms, they wore broad white hatbands so that other Union troops could distinguish them from guerrillas.

When they reported for enlistment, the authorities decided whether each man was loyal or not. If not, he and his property could be subject to seizure or assessment of financial penalties. As a result, General Order No. 19 also had the effect of driving many Missourians to join with recruiters such as Colonel Porter rather than be forced to join the EMM. Perhaps this explains Porter's persistence, in the face of incessant Federal pursuit, in continuing his recruiting efforts.

With the route south blocked by Guitar, Porter returned to the northeastern counties for more recruits. His men sacked Paris, Missouri, in Monroe County on July 30. They moved on to Newark on August 1, where they drove men of the Eleventh Cavalry MSM from their camp. The Federals took refuge in a brick church for an hour and a half before surrendering. Porter lost eight killed and thirteen wounded; the Federals lost four dead and seven wounded. The next day, a party of Rebels raided Canton, Missouri, where they killed one man and took weapons and ammunition. As they rode through the countryside, Porter's force swelled to nearly two thousand men, but only about a quarter were armed. The rest were awaiting word to make their way south to the Confederate army.

Union troops doggedly pursued Porter. "The militia," one of Porter's men wrote, "was crowding us on every side." Colonel John McNeil led a force composed of Shaffer's men from Merrill's Horse, a detachment of the Second Missouri Cavalry; detachments of the First, Ninth and Eleventh Cavalry MSM; a detachment of the Third Iowa Volunteer Infantry; and artillery (including a section from the Third Indiana Battery that fought at Moore's Mill). Altogether, the Federals had over one thousand heavily armed men. On August 6, 1862, Porter stopped at Kirksville to give battle.

General John McNeil. McNeil pursued and defeated Confederate colonel Joseph C. Porter in northeast Missouri. McNeil provoked international outrage by executing ten Confederate prisoners in retaliation for the killing of a Union civilian informant. *Library of Congress.*

1862: Guerrillas Fill the Void

As McNeil approached the town from the northeast, he could see nothing of the enemy, "except one man in the cupola of the court-house who retired at the bidding of a Sharp's rifle." Lieutenant Joseph Cowdrey, of Merrill's Horse, volunteered to take ten men into town to draw their fire and thus to disclose their position. Cowdrey's party rode into town, through the square and back out—with Porter's men firing at them the whole time. Two of the men were mortally wounded and three others slightly wounded, but his mission was successful. McNeil ordered the attack.

The Confederates were in the houses and cornfields on the edge of town. The artillery opened fire. It made many of the new recruits "very nervous, they never before having heard anything of the kind." The Federals charged into the town, and that began a house-to-house fight. One of Porter's men, R.K. Phillips of Ralls County, described the action:

> *I went back to my men, told them to follow me, and we dashed through that corn in somewhat of a hurry until the stable was reached, where we gave the advancing enemy four or five rounds. We then went through a large frame house, through the court-house and behind a picket fence we came up to our company. We fired a round or two and dropped back to another company, but the Federals were flanking us and we broke ranks and took to the brush. Here we were safe, as the enemy came no further.*

McNeil lost 6 killed and 33 wounded. Porter's losses were disastrous: over 100 dead, 200 wounded and 250 prisoners. Among the prisoners were 15 men who had previously been paroled by Union authorities. According to the terms of their parole, they agreed not to take up arms against the United States upon penalty of death. McNeil reported, "I enforced the penalty of the bond by ordering them shot." These men were fighting under a commander who had a commission from the Confederate government, not a self-appointed guerrilla like Quantrill. McNeil said that they had been captured before and they therefore violated a parole, not a loyalty oath. (McNeil paroled the other prisoners.) There was apparently no trial or appeal to higher headquarters. This was the beginning of a series of executions that led to McNeil being one of the most controversial and hated figures of the war.

And indeed he took the next step toward such notoriety two days later. Porter's second in command, Frisby McCullough, fell ill immediately after the Kirksville battle. He left the main force after declining an escort and was captured the next day by Missouri militia while resting in a grove of trees. The militiamen put him on a supply train headed to Kirksville. He arrived there on August 8. McNeil had him court-martialed as a guerrilla and an outlaw because, although he claimed to be a lieutenant colonel, he had no commission from the Confederate government. That was true; he had received his rank through an election of his men—a common method of selecting officers during the war. He was tried, found guilty and shot, all in the same day he reached town.

Porter was undeterred by the defeat at Kirksville. Although he avoided further major military action, he had one more raid to make. On September 12, Porter led about three hundred men into Palmyra to draw attention away from the recruits he was sending south to cross the Missouri River. They took the town completely by surprise. The two sides exchanged a few desultory shots, but the capture was complete in fifteen minutes. Porter freed fifty Confederate prisoners.

His men also took a sixty-year-old civilian, Andrew Allsman, as a prisoner. The local secessionists regarded Allsman as "a notorious crone, who haunted the provost marshal's office and made himself particularly obnoxious to Southern people by sending troops out after them or their stock." The next day, Colonel McNeil again surprised the Rebels in camp, this time near Newark. He scattered Porter's command into the woods. When the guerrillas reassembled, Allsman was gone. No one stepped forward to account for what had happened to Allsman, but there is little doubt that one of Porter's men killed him.

McNeil believed that an example should be made to deter such kidnappings. Although he may have strongly suspected that Allsman was already dead, he published an open letter in the *Palmyra Courier* to Colonel Porter demanding Allsman's return within ten days, or he would have ten Confederate prisoners shot in retaliation. He also gave a copy of the letter to Porter's wife, who lived nearby and whom he believed was in communication with her husband. Allsman was not returned, likely having already been killed a few weeks before.

McNeil had ten prisoners selected at random for execution at Palmyra. The story circulated among Southern sympathizers that the wife of one of the unlucky men went to Provost Marshal William Strachan, accompanied by one of her little daughters, to beg for her husband's life. Strachan agreed, but only if she provided sexual favors to him. She complied while the daughter waited outside, and Strachan substituted another man in her husband's place.

1862: Guerrillas Fill the Void

With the ten days up and Allsman not returned, the Federals carried out McNeil's threat. There was no claim that these men had committed any especially heinous crime, that they were somehow involved in Allsman's abduction or even that they had violated their parole.

The *Palmyra Courier* carried a full account of the incident. The story was reprinted by the Confederate *Memphis Appeal* and came to the attention of General Sterling Price, then serving in the army in Mississippi. He had a staff officer forward the clipping to President Jefferson Davis, with a request that he demand the surrender of McNeil or retaliate by executing a similar number of Union prisoners. On November 17, Davis issued an order to that effect to the Confederate commander of the Trans-Mississippi Department, General Theophilus Holmes. Holmes duly transmitted the message to Union lines. He received no response, and he took no further action.

News of the Palmyra Massacre, as it came to be called, spread abroad. London newspapers condemned the executions. The *New York Times* wrote a lengthy article on December 1 condemning the "execrations of the act of General McNeil." But it was careful to point out that McNeil was "not an officer of the National Army, nor has he any connection with the Government of the United States. He belongs to the 'Home Guard' of the State of Missouri, an organization which exists solely under State authority for local defense against lawless marauders in the rebel service, and is outside the control of the National Government…It was an affair between lawless, unorganized and unauthorized parties on both sides."

William Strachan, of all people, wrote a spirited defense of McNeil in a letter to the editors of the *Times*. "Numerous" citizens of Clarke, Lewis and Shelby Counties sent a letter to President Lincoln recounting the depredations of guerrillas throughout north Missouri. They commended McNeil's actions as "a stroke absolutely necessary" to deter guerrillas from killing civilians, looting and robbing loyal citizens. The signers claimed that the act "achieved its desired purpose."

While the level of guerrilla violence in northeast Missouri did decline, the violence in Missouri as a whole had yet to reach its crescendo. New and even more gruesome incidents were in store for the next two years.

Porter had one last skirmish in 1862. He led about 300 men to Portland, on the Missouri River in southeast Callaway County. There, the steamboat *Emilie* stopped to drop off 2 passengers. The guerrillas were hiding in the woodpile. When the boat landed, they ambushed it and compelled the captain to unload the deck freight. A total of 170 recruits boarded for the trip across the river. That was all who crossed, however. Federal cavalry caught up with the rest before the *Emilie* returned. The cavalry drove the Rebels away from the steamboat landing and chased them up the north bank of the river, killing 7.

Porter eventually crossed the Missouri River and made his way back to Arkansas. He made his last trip to Missouri in January 1863 as part of a force commanded by General John Marmaduke. Porter was shot in the leg and hand at a battle in Hartville, Missouri, on January 11, 1863. He survived for six weeks, finally dying of his wounds on February 18, 1863, at Batesville, Arkansas.

Chapter 4

Who Were the Guerrillas?

POLITICS, REVENGE AND MURDER

The guerrilla war in Missouri was, as one historian put, truly a "people's war." The bands were raised informally and sprang up for the most part as a response to local conditions, not on orders from a governmental authority. There were some exceptions—Confederate officers sent to Missouri to recruit soldiers for the regular army operated as guerrillas while the men were in the state. And the guerrillas, with a few notable exceptions, operated entirely independent of army authority or orders.

Why did these men turn to guerrilla warfare in Missouri?

There was an obvious political motive, especially in the first two years of the war. Many of the men who would later become guerrillas joined the Missouri State Guard in 1861 because they believed that the state needed defending from Nathaniel Lyon, Franz Sigel and his German American immigrants, John Frémont and a Union takeover. Many of Price's soldiers, once the Missouri State Guard left, and even more so after the defeat at Pea Ridge, simply returned home.

Apart from the political component, many men (particularly those in western Missouri) believed that the only way to defend their families and property from the depredations committed by Union troops, especially Kansas soldiers such those led by Jim Lane and Doc Jennison, was to take up arms as guerrillas. There was no Confederate army left to provide protection from marauding Federals. The Union commanders recognized the baleful influence of the Jayhawkers but were not successful in controlling their excesses.

This may explain why many of the guerrillas were young men from relatively well-to-do families. Their families were slave owners. Part of the measure of prosperity in a slave state like Missouri was the ownership of slaves who were, as peculiar as it sounds today, property. When the Jayhawkers freed their slaves and took them back to Kansas, they were not only taking the persons who worked their farms but also the basis for their wealth and status.

In addition, Mark Geiger has shown that many of the guerrillas' families lost their homes to foreclosure. As the leading citizens of their counties, they borrowed money to finance Price's army, pledging their farms as collateral. In exchange, they received bonds issued by Governor Jackson's Missouri government that were supposed to be paid by the Confederate government. When General Curtis drove Price from the state and defeated the Confederate army at Pea Ridge, there was little hope of repayment of the bonds. But the mortgages on the secessionists' farms were not affected because the loans they secured were made by the banks to the property owners, not to the government. Union sympathizers took over the banks. When the loans went into default, the Union-owned banks proceeded to foreclose on the properties. Thus, many leading secessionist families were ruined financially.

As the war entered 1862, politics and ideology became less important, and revenge came to the fore.

Cole Younger's experience was typical of many guerrillas. His father, Henry, was a prominent farmer and merchant, and the former mayor of Harrisonville. After the war, Cole wrote that his father, "though a slave-owner…had never been in sympathy with secession, believing, as it turned out, that it meant the death of slavery. He was for the Union, in spite of his natural inclinations to sympathy with the South." But on July 20, 1862, Union soldiers stopped Henry's buggy while he was returning from Kansas City. His body was found later lying in the road. Cole joined Quantrill's guerrillas. He took out his revenge by hunting down and ambushing the militiamen he believed responsible for his father's murder.

Whether men joined the guerrillas for revenge or for other reasons, the Union depredations fueled their anger and ultimately the viciousness of the war. The two sides traded atrocities, with each new depredation calling for a like response. The cycle of violence that started before the war continued and escalated as each year passed.

Who Were the Guerrillas?

While many guerrillas had what they and their sympathetic chroniclers regarded as just reasons for warring on Union soldiers and civilians, many—particularly later in the war—became guerrillas for the loot and the thrill of combat and killing. In a no-quarter war, these men went beyond simply killing in an ambush or a fight with Federal troops. They killed for the sake of killing. They were not content with just killing soldiers or civilians; they scalped and mutilated their bodies. What was considered "fiendish" at the beginning of the war paled beside the atrocities that were committed later.

WILLIAM QUANTRILL

William Clarke Quantrill was the most famous Missouri guerrilla, then and now. He was born in Canal Dover, Ohio, in 1837. His father was a schoolteacher. Quantrill taught school beginning at age sixteen in Ohio, Illinois and Indiana. In 1857, he moved to Kansas. In 1858, Quantrill traveled to Salt Lake City, Utah. He returned the next year and lived for a time in Lawrence. He also taught school near Osawatomie. During his time in Kansas, Quantrill apparently rode with both Jayhawkers and Border Ruffians. In 1860, he was charged with horse stealing. He left the state for Missouri.

Quantrill returned to Kansas to lead a Jayhawker raid, along with five abolitionists, on a large farm near Blue Springs, Missouri. They were planning to steal slaves from Morgan Walker, a prominent slave owner, and take them to Kansas. Pretending to reconnoiter Walker's farm, Quantrill instead told him of the impending raid. He returned to his companions and led them back to the farm—into an ambush.

William Clarke Quantrill. Quantrill was already well known in western Missouri by early 1862. The raid he led on Lawrence, Kansas, in 1863, in which more than 150 men were killed and the town was reduced to ruins, made Quantrill the most notorious guerrilla of the war. *The State Historical Society of Missouri, Columbia.*

One of the raiders was killed immediately. Two others were hunted down and shot, one of them by Quantrill himself. The others escaped to Kansas.

After first being threatened as a Jayhawker, Quantrill became a local hero to the slave-owning community when he convinced them that he was from Maryland and that he had betrayed his fellow raiders as revenge for the killing of his brother by free-soilers in Kansas. But Quantrill was never in Maryland, and he had no brother. He never gave any other explanation for his actions. In any event, he was firmly on the pro-Southern side by the time the war began.

Quantrill was a charismatic leader. Years after the war, Frank James still marveled at meeting him: "I will never forget the first time I saw Quantrill. He was nearly six feet in height, rather thin, his hair and mustache was sandy and he was full of life and a jolly fellow. He had none of the air of bravado or the desperado about him, [but] he was a demon in battle."

WILLIAM "BLOODY BILL" ANDERSON

William Anderson Jr., who became known as "Bloody Bill" for the extraordinary viciousness of his conduct, was born in Kentucky in 1839. He had a brother Jim, who also became a guerrilla, and three sisters— Mary Ellen, Josephine and Janie. The Anderson family lived in Huntsville, Missouri. In 1855, Anderson's father, William Sr., staked a claim near Council Grove, Kansas, when the new state opened up for settlement. He moved the family to the new homestead in 1857.

Anderson's father owned 320 acres of farmland, a grocery store and a freighting business that catered to travelers on the Santa Fe Trail. Although the family was reasonably well off for the times, Bill was not able to stay out of trouble. In 1860, he started his own "business"—stealing horses in Missouri and selling them in Kansas. In late 1861, Bill joined with a local merchant, Arthur Inghram Baker, who had fallen on hard times, to Jayhawk in Missouri. The expedition failed, however, and Baker went back to selling whiskey and supplies to travelers on the Santa Fe Trail.

Bill continued his horse-stealing ways. He did not pretend to have any higher motive for bushwhacking. He told one friend, "I don't care any more than you for the South…but there is a lot of money in this business."

Baker began to call on Bill's oldest sister, Mary Ellen, but left her to marry another woman. The elder Anderson saw the marriage as a betrayal and insult to the family. He was going to get even. On May 12, 1862, William

Who Were the Guerrillas?

William "Bloody Bill" Anderson. Anderson terrorized north central Missouri in 1864. He ordered the killing of twenty-three unarmed Union soldiers at Centralia and led the ambush later that day in which a battalion of the Thirty-ninth Missouri Infantry was wiped out. After killing Anderson in October 1864, Union troops found a necklace with fifty-three scalps on his body. *B. J. George Collection, the State Historical Society of Missouri, Columbia.*

Sr. took his shotgun to Baker's house to vindicate his daughter's honor. When William Sr. broke in, he ran up the stairs to confront Baker in his bedroom. Baker stepped out with his own shotgun and, with one blast, killed his assailant. Baker knew that William Sr.'s son was a dangerous man to have angry with him. He got the authorities to charge Bill with horse stealing. Bill and his brother Jim fled to Missouri. Their three sisters followed shortly.

But on July 3, Bill and Jim returned. An accomplice fooled Baker into opening his store to get some whiskey out of the cellar, supposedly for a Fourth of July celebration. Baker went to the cellar to draw the whiskey, but when he turned around, there were Bill and Jim Anderson. Baker pulled out his revolver and shot Jim in the thigh, but Bill shot back. Baker lay wounded in the cellar. The Andersons also shot Baker's son-in-law, who had gone to the store with him, and dumped him in the cellar, too. They piled boxes and barrels on the trapdoor and set the building on fire. Baker killed himself before the fire could do it. The son-in-law survived just long enough to tell what happened and died the next day.

The Andersons fled to Missouri to become full-time guerrillas. In 1862, Bill Anderson operated in southeastern Jackson County. He was not too careful in picking out his victims, earning a humiliating rebuke from Quantrill for attacking Southern sympathizers as well as Unionists. He then shifted his activities eastward, to Johnson County. By 1863, Anderson was a self-proclaimed "captain" of the First Kansas Guerrillas. One of his chief lieutenants was nineteen-year-old Archie Clement from Kingsville, Johnson County. "Little Archie," as he was known, was barely five feet tall. He was, however, one of the most vicious of the men in Anderson's band. Clement became one of young Jesse James's best friends among the guerrillas. Both Anderson and Clement became famous for scalping their victims. Anderson was supposed to have kept his victims' scalps on a silk cord worn around his neck. At the time of his death, Anderson's necklace had fifty-three scalps on it.

Anderson and his men participated in Quantrill's raid on Lawrence, but he earned his lasting fame in 1864.

GEORGE TODD

George Todd was a Scot. He is said to have killed a man there and to have fled to Canada. Later, Todd turned up in Jackson County. Todd was a bridge mason for railroad contractors before the war. He joined Quantrill as one of his most trusted lieutenants in 1861. Unlike some guerrillas who sought to cloak their activities in a veneer of lawfulness by claiming they were acting on orders from the Confederate government, Todd declared, "You need not consider me a Confederate officer. I intend to follow bushwhacking as long as I live."

George Todd, from John N. Edwards, *Noted Guerrillas* (1877). Todd was one of Quantrill's principal lieutenants. He took over leadership of the band in 1864, after he accused Quantrill of cowardice for advising against an attack on Federal troops in Fayette. The attack turned out to be a disaster for the guerrillas. Todd was killed at the Battle of the Little Blue in 1864. *The State Historical Society of Missouri, Columbia.*

Todd was ambitious. He took over the leadership of Quantrill's men in the summer of 1864, when the latter seemed to lose the aggressiveness that impressed his followers. Todd met his death on October 21, 1864, on the Little Blue River, near Independence—ironically, not as a guerrilla, but as a scout in Jo Shelby's cavalry division of General Price's army.

DAVE POOLE AND CHARLES FLETCHER TAYLOR

Dave Poole (also spelled Pool) was from Lexington, Missouri, in the heart of Little Dixie. He was known as a prankster among his fellow guerrillas, but his humor was of the most macabre kind. On one occasion, his men trapped nine Union soldiers in a schoolhouse and killed them all. Poole propped the bodies up in chairs and proceeded to "teach" them. He proclaimed the pupils were very good at sitting and listening to him. After the Battle of Centralia, Poole went along the line of Union bodies, jumping from corpse to corpse. When another guerrilla protested that what he was doing was inhuman, Poole replied, "If they are dead I can't hurt them. I cannot count them good without stepping on them. When I got my foot on one this way I know I've got him."

Left to right: Archie Clement, Dave Poole and Bill Hendricks. This photograph was probably taken in Sherman, Texas, on Christmas Day 1863. Note the multiple revolvers each man carried. *The State Historical Society of Missouri, Columbia.*

Charles Fletcher "Fletch" Taylor was one of Quantrill's early recruits. He scouted Lawrence before the 1863 raid. The following winter in Texas, Taylor shot and killed a Confederate officer. When Quantrill tried to arrest him, Taylor took some men and went out "on his own hook." Returning from a raid in 1864, militiamen ambushed Taylor's band. Taylor suffered a shotgun wound to his right arm, which had to be amputated. After the war, Taylor lived in Joplin, Missouri. He became a wealthy owner of lead mines in Jasper County. Once former Confederates were franchised again, he was elected to the Missouri General Assembly. Fletcher later moved to California, where he died in 1912, at age seventy.

CLIFF HOLTZCLAW

Clifton D. "Cliff" Holtzclaw lived in Howard County, Missouri. He was born in 1830. He joined Price's Missouri State Guard in 1861 but was captured at Boonville by Lyon's forces. He later rejoined Price in time for the siege of Lexington in September 1861. Although he was a noted guerrilla leader, Holtzclaw was unusual in that he had an actual officer's commission in the Confederate army—a fact that he pointed out to Federal authorities several times in letters. He was wounded at Pea Ridge. Holtzclaw went to Mississippi with Price after Pea Ridge and served in the Sixth Missouri Infantry.

In 1863, the Confederate high command sent Holtzclaw back to Howard County to recruit. He led a band of guerrillas in north central Missouri for the next two years. In September 1863, Lieutenant Joseph Street went to the farm owned by Holtzclaw's father, James. He demanded that the elder Holtzclaw lead him to his son's hideout. But one of Street's men "accidentally" shot the old man in the head, killing him instantly.

In August 1864, Holtzclaw joined forces with Bill Anderson. His men were at the Battle of Centralia but apparently were not among those who sacked the town and murdered twenty-three unarmed Federal soldiers at the train station. In early October, Holtzclaw led his band into Fayette, Howard County, to rob the bank and to catch a particular Union officer: Lieutenant Joseph Street. They succeeded in stealing $14,000 from the bank. Street was killed in the ensuing firefight.

Holtzclaw, along with other guerrilla leaders, met Price in October 1864 at Boonville. Holtzclaw's men joined Shelby's cavalry. He helped Shelby capture Carrollton on October 17. Perhaps satisfied that he had taken his revenge on his father's killers, Holtzclaw stopped his guerrilla activities in 1865 and moved out of Missouri.

SAMUEL HILDEBRAND

During the war, Samuel Hildebrand became as well known in southeastern Missouri as Quantrill was in western Missouri. Hildebrand was born in 1836 and lived in St. Francois County. By September 1861, Federal reports described him as one of the "notorious leaders of the rebels" and a "notorious bushwhacker." Hildebrand, on the other hand, claimed that he remained neutral until Union vigilantes hanged his brother Frank. He had his revenge, however, when he stalked and killed their leader,

Who Were the Guerrillas?

Firmin McIvaine. Hildebrand lost two other brothers to Federal action. In July 1862, soldiers killed his older brother, Washington. Later that same month, Federal cavalry burned Hildebrand's house and killed his younger brother, Henry.

He was chased out of the state in 1862 and claimed to have received a commission as a Confederate major while in Arkansas. Hildebrand led numerous raids in southeastern Missouri from 1863 through 1865. He claimed to have killed over eighty men. At one point, Federal officers wrote that Union men in St. Francois County were "frightened and will abandon their crops and everything, because they know that Hildebrand declared that he will never stop until he had everyone's life. He is one of the most bloodthirsty rebels in the country."

Hildebrand served briefly as a scout for Price's 1864 raid but returned to his guerrilla activities when Price was defeated. After the war, Hildebrand continued his violent ways, resorting to robbery and murder. In 1870, he published the *Autobiography of Samuel S. Hildebrand: The Renowned Missouri Bushwhacker*. He moved to Illinois, where he was killed while resisting arrest.

FRANK AND JESSE JAMES

Frank and Jesse James were born in Clay County, Missouri. Their parents, Robert and Zerelda James, like many Missourians, were originally from Kentucky. They moved to Missouri to grow hemp. Hemp was a major cash crop in Missouri and helped connect it to the South because its primary use was to bind cotton bales. The James family had six slaves in 1850, including "Aunt" Charlotte and five others ages two to eleven. Charlotte would remain with the family until her death well after the war. In addition to farming, Robert was a well-known, charismatic preacher who organized the longest and most successful camp meeting revival in the county in 1849. The next year, he left the family for California, ostensibly to preach, but the neighbors suspected he was, like many at the time, drawn to seeking riches in the gold rush. Robert never got a chance to do much preaching or to get rich. He died within months of arriving there.

Zerelda was a strong-willed woman. She had to be to survive as a widow running a farm in rural Missouri. She did not remain a widow long. She married Benjamin Simms in 1852. It was not a happy union. Simms died in 1854. Zerelda married for a third time in 1855. Her husband, and the children's stepfather, was Reuben Samuel, a doctor originally from Kentucky.

Samuel gave up the practice of medicine, however, to help run the farm. And the farm was successful. By 1860, Zerelda and Reuben owned seven slaves—Charlotte and six others ranging in age from one to eighteen.

When the war came, Frank joined the Missouri State Guard. He fought at Wilson's Creek in August and at Lexington in September. He fell sick with measles and was left behind in Springfield when Price's men withdrew to northern Arkansas. After recovering from his illness, Frank came home a combat veteran at age eighteen. He could not stay away from the excitement of war. In 1863, he joined a local band of guerrillas led by Fernando Scott.

The guerrillas told Jesse he was too young to become a member, but he was allowed to load extra cylinders for their revolvers. The job was a dangerous one. (One story says that Jesse accidentally shot the tip of his finger off at this task.) Navy revolvers, the guerrillas' preferred weapon, did not use single cartridges like modern pistols. Rather, they had to be loaded with gunpowder and ball, rammed home, sealed with grease and fitted with a percussion cap made of fulminate of mercury. Guerrillas carried extra cylinders with them so they could reload in a firefight by replacing the empty one with a loaded one.

On May 19, 1863, Scott's guerrillas lured Lieutenant Louis Gravenstein and four men of the Twenty-fifth Missouri Infantry out of their post at Missouri City, in southeastern Clay County. When Gravenstein and his men approached a bridge over the Fishing River, Scott's men opened fire, killing one soldier and wounding another. When Gravenstein tried to surrender, he was shot dead. The guerrillas then rode into Missouri City and looted it.

The attack sparked a Federal manhunt. Frank, among others, was recognized as one of the men involved. Unionist militia made for the Samuel household. Jesse was working in the fields when the militia arrived. They beat and dragged him to the house. The Union commander demanded that Reuben tell them where Frank and the guerrilla band were hiding. Reuben said he did not know. The officers did not believe him "and at once procured a rope, placed it around his neck, and gave him one good swing." As Zerelda was cursing the militia, they asked Reuben once again where the guerrillas' camp was. "[Reuben's] memory brightened up, and he concluded to reveal the hiding place of the rebels. He led the boys into the woods a short distance, and there, squatted upon the ground in a dense thicket, was discovered the whole band." The militia killed five of Scott's men as they scrambled to escape. Not long after this, Frank joined Quantrill. He participated in the murderous raid on Lawrence and Quantrill's other actions in 1863.

Left to right: Charles Fletcher Taylor, Frank James and Jesse James. Jesse and Frank joined Taylor in May 1864. This photograph was taken before Taylor lost his right arm in August 1864. *The State Historical Society of Missouri, Columbia.*

Jesse was finally judged old enough to become a guerrilla in May 1864. He still had not yet reached his sixteenth birthday. Jesse's first guerrilla leader was Fletch Taylor, one of Quantrill's former lieutenants. Jesse became best friends with another young man, Archie Clement. On August 13, 1864, Jesse was shot in the chest by a German farmer from whom he was attempting to steal a saddle. Remarkably, he recovered in time to join Taylor, Anderson, Todd and his brother Frank near Centralia, Missouri, on September 23. Both would participate in the Battle of Centralia on September 27, where the guerrillas ambushed and wiped out a pursuing Federal battalion. Neither Frank nor Jesse ever admitted to being present earlier in the day when Anderson's men shot and killed twenty-three unarmed soldiers taken off a train at the Centralia railroad station.

Frank and Jesse, of course, survived the war. They became famous, not for being Civil War guerrillas, but for being postwar bank and train robbers.

ALVIN COBB

Alvin Cobb was one of the most colorful guerrillas, although his career was short. Cobb was from Montgomery County in central Missouri. He led several attacks in that vicinity and fought alongside Porter at the Battle of Moore's Mill. The *Liberty Tribune* provided the only known description of Cobb:

> *He is about forty-five years old—six feet tall, symmetrically formed and weighing about one hundred and eighty pounds—his right arm has been cut off about the wrist. He has an iron hook fastened to his arm by which he holds his bridle. He dresses awkwardly and oddly—he has a savage looking countenance, (what can be seen of it) his hair hangs down to his shoulders, and his face is covered with beard, which is long—reaching to his waist. His eyes are grey and piercing. He looks but little like a military man. To say the least of him, he is a "hard looking customer."*

After Moore's Mill, Cobb's men operated independently in Montgomery, Callaway and Audrain Counties. At one point, he led his band into Portland, a Callaway County river town, supposedly singing "Dixie." The guerrillas demanded food and rode away. Cobb's men went south for the winter of 1862–63 but returned briefly the next year to their familiar area of operations. Sometime after 1863, Cobb went to Oklahoma Territory and joined Stand Waitie's Cherokee brigade. He survived the war and apparently moved to California.

HENRY TAYLOR

Henry Taylor (no relation to Fletch Taylor) was born in Kentucky and moved to Vernon County in southwest Missouri in 1849. He was a merchant and sheriff at Nevada City. Taylor joined the Missouri State Guard in 1861 and fought at Carthage, Wilson's Creek and Drywood Creek. Like many others who became guerrillas, Taylor left the Missouri State Guard on its retreat to Arkansas in late 1861. Within two weeks, he had organized a guerrilla band and raided Fort Scott, Kansas.

In April 1862, Missouri militia captured Taylor at his father-in-law's house in Montevallo, Vernon County. He was taken to Fort Scott, where he was paroled. In the summer of 1863, Taylor was "exchanged" and went back to bushwhacking. Taylor spent the winter of 1863–64 in Sherman, Texas, with Quantrill's men. In 1864, he returned to Missouri, but by the end of the summer, he had joined Shelby's division on Price's raid. Taylor once again left for Texas when winter came. During the spring of 1865, Taylor rode with Dave Poole and Archie Clement. He surrendered with Poole on May 20, 1865.

Taylor left Missouri after the war. He lived in Illinois and Nebraska. Taylor came back to Vernon County, where he was once again elected sheriff in 1872. Among his postwar accomplishments, Taylor helped to lay out the resort town of Eureka Springs, Arkansas.

Chapter 5

Attacked by Both Sides

Civil War Life in Rural Missouri

CIVILIANS AS VICTIMS AND SUPPORTERS

If she had lived in one of the larger towns or cities, such as St. Louis, Elvira Scott would not have had to endure the murderous visits of either guerrillas or marauding Federal troops. But Elvira Scott lived in Miami, Missouri, a little town on the Missouri River in Saline County northeast of Lexington.

The Kansas Cavalry, known as Red Legs for the red leather gaiters they wore, paid Miami a visit, ostensibly looking for bushwhackers. They demanded food, which Scott "did not dare to refuse them." They threatened to steal her aged horse, Charley. Scott managed to talk them out of that and thought that she had survived the visit when she heard her neighbor screaming at her to come to the front yard. One of the Red Legs was shoving her husband, John, before him with a gun. She got between them, but the soldier, who was drunk, kept pushing them toward the house and swearing that he would shoot. Scott managed to calm the man down enough to allow John to get his horse. But the troops took John and four other men of the village as hostages. They were later released. John Scott and his companions were lucky. Whether the men the Red Legs found lived or died seemed a random choice: these men went unharmed; others were killed.

Just two days later, while sitting down to dinner, Scott saw a company of men dressed in blue again riding into town, firing their guns. These were not Federals but a band of guerrillas wearing uniforms they had either stolen or taken from dead Union soldiers. They also gathered the men of the town into a group. One of the prisoners had been in the militia and still wore his uniform. Scott wrote in her diary: "After they got him I suppose he felt his fate was sealed. He broke guard & ran down the hollow by the warehouse. Three of them pursued, & the firing was at him. He refused to surrender & was killed almost instantly."

The guerrillas were "nicely dressed" and carried "belts full of pistols." They were "a reckless, daring set of men, ready to sell their lives as dearly as possible, knowing that they would get no quarter if captured." Scott talked to some of them, asking why they came, especially knowing that Union troops might well retaliate if the residents provided any help. "He answered it was nothing when we got used to it; that he had been hung three times & that if the Federals burned houses & shot people they would burn & shoot too."

As historian Michael Fellman put it, the guerrillas' method and purpose was terror. They usually operated in an area well known to them. Thus, they could strike quickly and make a getaway to hideouts in the bush where Federal soldiers could not find them. They could choose their targets— neighbors whom they knew to be Unionists or merely against whom they had nursed a grudge. And they struck with ferocious violence.

Guerrilla Depredations—Stealing Horses, from *Harper's Weekly*, December 24, 1864. *Library of Congress.*

The guerrillas could attack whole towns, like Miami, or they could strike against helpless individuals, like women living alone because their husbands and sons were either away in the army or dead. The victims might know who their attackers were but be afraid to tell the authorities because of the threat of reprisals.

Sometimes the guerrillas used brute force, as when they burst in Obidiah and Nancy Leavitt's store. Obidiah tried to resist, but the three men shot him in the back. Nancy took a shotgun and held them off for about an hour. Then they persuaded her to give up, promising that "they would not bother me or my husband any more—and that they would not take my critters." But they lied. When she let them back in the house, one grabbed her and another shot her wounded husband in the head, killing him. They stole the Leavitts' "critters" and rode away.

At other times, the guerrillas used trickery. One night in late October 1864, Frank and Jesse James went to the home of a Mr. Baynes, a known Unionist. The James boys were wearing captured Union uniform coats. They knocked on the door, claiming to be lost Union soldiers asking for directions. Baynes came out into his yard and directed them to the main road. Frank and Jesse pulled out their pistols and shot Baynes five times. They pulled the same trick with the same result on a man named Farran. They went to the Rogers house, but the ruse failed to work. Rogers would not come out, and they left.

Many of the guerrillas' victims were targeted—not surprising, given that most bands operated in and near home territory where their members and the militia chasing them both lived. For example, on the way to Olathe in September 1862, members of Quantrill's guerrillas—apparently including Cole Younger—stopped at the John Judy farm just east of town. John Judy was the son of Reason Judy, a prominent citizen, Unionist and Missouri militia officer who had fought at the Battle of Lone Jack. John was Reason's oldest son. Another son, James, age eighteen, was at home when the guerrillas arrived that day. Both Judy brothers had enlisted in the Twelfth Kansas Infantry and were to leave the next day to join their unit. A neighbor later told what happened:

> *Mrs. Judy and a neighbor girl staying there were still sitting up, the brothers having retired, when the house was surrounded and ten or fifteen men entered. They ordered the two brothers to get up and dress at once, and then ransacked the house for any valuables they might find… "If you have much Union about you, better work it off by crying, and we'll give you cause enough," said one…* [T]*hey ordered the brothers to mount behind two of*

Attacked by Both Sides

their men and galloped away. Mrs. Judy left for a neighbor's a half mile away, as soon as they had gone, and while on the road heard the five shots that killed her husband and his brother...John Judy had been shot once in the left eye and twice in the breast. His brother, James, once in the face and once in the breast.

Even families with Southern connections were sometimes treated roughly. Dicey Smith had two brothers in the Confederate army. She, like Reason Judy, lived in Cass County, where both guerrillas and Federals swept through with discouraging regularity. Her sister married a Northerner, and so her father spent most of his time with her. He had to hide in the cornfield when the guerrillas came, but the rest of her family was safe. She gave the guerrillas what food they had, but they wanted more. "Did we have food hidden? Was there any weapons or money in the house? Where were the men and did we have any livestock?" Once they left a grim reminder of the war behind: "Another day a band of Confederate soldiers came by with a Federal soldier tied to his horse. They did not stop, but when we went to feed our small pigs, there was the prisoner in the pig pen shot to death. We dragged him from the pen and Leah went to get Bob to help dig a grave. He had no identification of any kind, so no one ever knew who he was."

Guerrillas showed a special vengeance for German Americans, popularly known at the time as "Dutch." The Dutch were strong Unionists and antislavery partisans. In July 1863, Bill Anderson led forty men on a raid into a German stronghold in Lafayette County. Dave Poole, who was from the area, was especially virulent in his hatred of the "Dutch." They attacked the town of Concordia, with little success, because the residents withdrew to a blockhouse, a fortification—like a brick courthouse—the guerrillas could rarely breach. They did find four unfortunate members of the local EMM without arms and killed them.

Early in the war, the presence of large numbers of guerrillas, particularly in western and southwestern Missouri, caused many Union sympathizers simply to leave. Many Unionists living in Jackson County, for example, were gone by the end of 1861. Families that had nowhere else to go left their isolated farms and moved close to military posts at places like Pleasant Hill and Harrisonville in Cass County. It was a difficult existence, but at least there was some measure of protection.

For those who chose to remain on their farms, the army and militia provided little security against sudden strikes by bands of marauders who then melted into the wild. Even when Federal troops were present, they often

Atrocities of the Secessionists. This print from a German newspaper shows an attack on civilians by guerrillas. German immigrants were special targets of the guerrillas because of their ardent support of abolition of slavery. *From the Art Collection, WARS 57, The State Historical Society of Missouri, Columbia.*

were no less cruel than the guerrillas. The army, in the name of "foraging," could be just as devastating to a small farm as raiders from the bush.

The Unionists fled before the guerrillas, and the secessionists fled before the Federals. The land was "nearly forsaken." Large parts of some previously thriving towns were left devastated.

> *Westport* [near Kansas City] *was once a thriving town, with large stores, elegant private dwellings and a fine large hotel. Now soldiers are quartered in the dwellings and horses occupy the storerooms. The hotel was burned down three days ago. The houses are torn to pieces, plastering off, the mantles used to build fires, and doors unhinged. I presume the place will be burned as soon as the troops leave.*

As many as forty thousand refugees fled to St. Louis, the one city in the state safe from guerrilla attacks. General Halleck wrote, "Men, women, and children have alike been stripped and plundered. Thousands of such persons

70

are finding their way to this city barefooted, half clad, and in a destitute and starving condition." To cope with this influx, he ordered that assessments, totaling $10,000, be levied upon persons "known to be hostile to the Union." When Samuel Engler sued to recover eighty boxes of candles confiscated to satisfy the assessment against him, Halleck ordered Engler arrested and banished from the state for interfering with the military.

In January 1863, Lincoln finally ordered the practice of assessments stopped because the board established to carry out the policy often acted on suspicion and unproven accusations and was plagued by accusations of corruption. Federal authorities did not revive assessments until Price's 1864 raid and further guerrilla attacks caused a new wave of refugees to flee to St. Louis.

The families of men who were serving in the Confederate army or who were in the bush with the guerrillas suffered at least as much as the families of Union soldiers and militia. But to say that the secessionist families were innocent victims would not be accurate. The guerrillas' families were, in fact, their most reliable supply line. Certainly, they could and did take clothes, weapons, ammunition, money and food from Union troops or Union sympathizers. But their wives and mothers were what sustained the ability to survive.

Guerrillas had no supply depots, quartermasters or procurement officers to buy the goods necessary to carry on a war. The key to their success was that they did not need such a formal system. They would simply slip into their homes and get them from their families.

General Thomas Ewing noted that guerrillas did not rely on regular supply lines for food or other necessities: "All of the people of the country, through fear or favor, feed them, and rarely give information as to their movements. Having all the inhabitants, by good will or compulsion, thus practically their friends, and being familiar with the fastness of the country wonderfully adapted by nature to guerrilla warfare, they have generally been able to elude the most energetic pursuit."

The guerrillas were, after all, fighting near home. They knew who could be trusted and who could not. They usually traveled in small bands that could easily be fed by one household. The women could sew their clothes and provide what food the farm could spare. And usually no one else would even know they were there.

Joseph Beilein tells of one guerrilla, Jim Rider from Livingston County, who regularly visited not only his own home but also those of two of his uncles, an aunt and two friends who lived nearby. He spent no more than one night at

Refugees from Northern Missouri Entering St. Louis, an 1864 illustration from *Harper's Pictorial History of the Civil War*. In 1862, Union commanders assessed Southern sympathizers for the cost of caring for civilians fleeing their farms from guerrillas. The practice was stopped in 1863 due to widespread corruption but resumed in 1864 when a new wave of refugees left their homes for the safety of the city. *Library of Congress.*

each place. The households were located in three different counties but near to the targets in central Missouri that Rider was known to have attacked.

Although both sides regarded women as noncombatants, by 1863, Ewing recognized that something had to be done to interrupt the supply line. In one such incident, he sent Federal cavalry from Kansas City to arrest

Mollie Grindstaff for holding stolen property and for aiding and abetting guerrillas. She was suspected of supplying guerrillas with clothing because she was thought to have received a large amount of cloth Quantrill's guerrillas had stolen in Shawneetown, Kansas.

The soldiers went first to the Mundy household. Grindstaff was there but claimed to be one of the Mundy sisters. One of the cavalrymen recognized her, however, from a picture he had taken from a guerrilla. The soldiers proceeded to search the house. They found forty shirts—far more than was needed for that household. And what is more, they were "guerrilla" shirts, the distinctive embroidered garment with large pockets to hold extra ammunition for navy revolvers. They arrested all the women present and took them back to Kansas City. The women included Bill Anderson's three sisters, Mary Ellen, Josephine and Janie. Around the same time, Federal soldiers also arrested Nannie Harris, Charity McCorkle Kerr, Armenia Crawford Selvey and Susan Crawford Van Dever—all of them related to guerrillas. These women were in a Kansas City jail when it collapsed on August 13, killing Josephine and severely injuring Mary Ellen. Their husbands and brothers were outraged that "innocent" women were jailed, let alone killed and maimed.

Although victims of a disastrous building failure, these women were not—as they were portrayed by their families—blameless bystanders. They were full-fledged participants in the guerrilla war. In the words of Leann Whites, they were the guerrillas' "female sustained...willing line of supply." General Ewing's recognition of the role of the guerrillas' female family members led him to recommend, and later to order, the wholesale depopulation of four and a half counties in western Missouri to eliminate the bushwhackers' base of operations.

SLAVES

Slavery was the flashpoint that plunged Missouri into the border war in the 1850s and into the Civil War along with other states. As a border state where slavery was an important aspect of its economy, Missouri was in an unusual position. It had not successfully seceded, despite Governor Claiborne Jackson's best efforts, due largely to the decisive action of General Nathaniel Lyon and a generally neutral (if not Unionist) population. Therefore, Lincoln's Emancipation Proclamation of January 1, 1863, did not apply to Missouri slaves. But to say that Missouri's slaves were not affected by the war would be to miss the mark by a wide margin.

The 1860 census showed that Missouri had 114,931 slaves living in the state. By 1863, that number had dropped to 73,811, a decline of 35 percent. To be sure, some masters sent their slaves out of state to be sold to work elsewhere after the war began, but the drop is best explained by the allure of freedom. The slaves liberated themselves by fleeing to Kansas, Iowa or Illinois. The numbers would drop even further in the next two years until Missouri freed all slaves.

Many men who escaped to Kansas enlisted in the Union army. When recruitment of slaves was finally permitted in Missouri, the men who enlisted automatically gained their freedom. Hundreds of men flocked to Benton Barracks in St. Louis. Some did so at considerable peril to themselves. Slaveholders in some areas of Little Dixie, with the tacit approval of local military officials, resumed slave patrols to prevent blacks from enlisting. Guerrillas, too, made a special effort to discourage enlistments by killing any slaves they found headed to the recruitment stations. But once in the army, former slaves could fight Confederate soldiers and guerrillas on more or less equal terms.

Those who did not or could not escape or enlist nevertheless could fight back against their masters. Just as white Southern sympathizers provided information to guerrillas about Union troop movements, slaves assisted Union forces with critical intelligence, often running a greater personal risk than their masters. A slave woman named Easter fled to the safety of Columbia when bushwhackers left a note threatening her for being a "notorious reporter…[I]f you are found in this county one month after receiving this notice you will pull a rope. You must take all your brood with you and skedaddle like hell." A sixty-seven-year-old black man told authorities that his master, Eli Bass—the owner of the largest plantation in Missouri—habitually harbored guerrillas such as Bill Anderson. "I knew [Anderson's] horse," he said, and "could tell his nicker."

The political convulsions that surrounded the eventual emancipation of Missouri slaves split the Unionists into several different groups. And what to do with the black refugees who flooded the Federal camps during the war was a problem that plagued Union commanders from the beginning. They vacillated between treating them as "contraband"—property that, if used to assist the rebellion, could be confiscated—and runaway slaves subject to being returned to bondage. Because Missouri was still a slave state, the issue was a source of constant political irritation.

General Halleck tried to keep the military neutral in such disputes. But his attempts to straddle a fine line between slave owners and antislavery groups

An unidentified former slave and Union soldier at Benton Barracks, St. Louis. Slaves who joined the army were given their freedom, although their families were not. Many slaveholders resisted having their "property" thus taken away from them. The guerrillas attacked and killed many slaves who tried to leave their masters to enlist. *Library of Congress.*

were not always successful. For example, a group of former slaves captured in southwest Missouri were brought to St. Louis, jailed and advertised for sale as "unclaimed property" in accordance with Missouri's slave code. Halleck stepped in to free them on the grounds that the federal law superseded state law in this respect. He said their owners could use the state courts to recover them if the captives were, in fact, not free.

Governor Gamble offered a plan to the legislature for gradual, compensated emancipation, but it did not pass over the opposition of abolitionists who argued for immediate emancipation. Lincoln hoped that the passage of gradual emancipation in Missouri would settle the sharp divisions within the party. An exasperated Lincoln wrote there were "those who are for the Union with, not without, slavery; those who are for it without, not with; those for it with or without, but prefer it with; and those for it with or without, but prefer it without. Among these, again, is a subdivision of those who are for gradual, but not for immediate, and those who are for immediate, but not gradual, extinction of slavery."

Gamble's plan, however, was ultimately overtaken by events. Lincoln authorized the recruitment of black troops in border states like Missouri in the spring of 1863. The first such unit was enlisted in southwest Missouri, although it was designated an Arkansas regiment. In November 1863, General Schofield issued orders that provided for the enlistment of "all able-bodied colored men, whether free or slaves," and that "all persons enlisted into the service shall forever thereafter be free." Owners who submitted an oath of allegiance and a deed of manumission would receive $300 in compensation. Disloyal owners would receive nothing.

Emancipation in Missouri finally came when the Radical legislature unconditionally abolished slavery in the state effective July 4, 1865. The slavery controversy that began with the birth of Missouri in 1820 and erupted into violence with the Kansas-Nebraska Act was ended. It meant freedom for African Americans in the state, but not yet equality.

Chapter 6
1863–1864: The Destruction of Lawrence and Order No. 11

GENERAL EWING'S PROBLEM

Guerrilla activity exploded in 1863. Beginning in March, there were seemingly constant clashes between Federal soldiers and bushwhackers throughout western Missouri, especially in the counties bordering Kansas. On March 1, George Todd, Cole Younger and Fletch Taylor made a daring raid on downtown Kansas City. They robbed residents, entered a saloon and shot several soldiers and stole thirty horses. On March 18, Younger and John McCorkle robbed a stagecoach between Kansas City and Independence. Four days later, Todd led an ambush of a Federal patrol near Independence.

On March 28, William Gregg, one of Quantrill's lieutenants, stopped the *Sam Gaty* near Sibley, in eastern Jackson County. He had word that Reverend Hugh Fisher was supposed to be on board with freed slaves from southeast Missouri whom he was taking to Kansas. The slaves were there, but Fisher did not make the trip. Sixty former slaves ran away in terror. The remaining twenty or so were lined up, and the guerrillas executed nine of them. They robbed the passengers and threw tons of army supplies into the river.

Federal troops flooded Jackson County, accompanied by a group of Red Legs, led by George Hoyt, one of John Brown's lawyers at his trial for the Harpers Ferry attack. They were supposed to be looking for the perpetrators of the *Sam Gaty* attack but spent most of their time pillaging. The Federals claim to have scattered seven guerrilla camps and killed seventeen bushwhackers, but it is just as likely that the dead were farmers who had nothing to do with the steamboat attack and whose only crime was to be Southern sympathizers.

May brought another round of guerrilla attacks—including one that led to a prominent role for one of its leaders, William Anderson. Anderson and a group of guerrillas rode deep into Kansas to attack the town of Council Grove, some 150 miles from the Missouri border. Anderson had lived in the area before the war. The raiders robbed and killed farmers and travelers along the Santa Fe Trail. Although it accomplished little of military value, the Council Grove raid heightened the fear of guerrilla raids among Kansans and proved that the state was vulnerable to such assaults.

The guerrillas kept up their attacks on steamboats. They fired on the *Fanny Ogden* on May 13 and on the *Magenta* on May 19 near Napoleon, east of Kansas City. They attacked the *Spread Eagle* on May 28 near Waverly, in northeastern Lafayette County. And the stagecoach between Lexington and Kansas City was robbed two more times, on May 15 and 17.

General John Schofield sought a special type of officer for the District of the Border, which encompassed the western counties of Missouri and the eastern counties of Kansas. This was the most sensitive and contentious part of Schofield's territory. Schofield needed a man who could handle a situation that called as much on an officer's political skills as his military prowess.

And so in June 1863, Thomas Ewing Jr. received his general's stars and the command of the District of the Border. Ewing was not a military man. He was a transplanted Kansan and a lawyer by trade. His father, Thomas Sr., was a senator from Ohio and secretary of the interior under President Zachary Taylor. Ewing himself had served as Taylor's private secretary at the age of twenty. Ewing's brother-in-law, William T. Sherman, was a military man, if not a particularly successful one prior to the war. Ewing and Sherman were close because Sherman had lived with the Ewing family from the age of eight and later married Ewing's sister.

In 1856, Ewing opened a law practice in Leavenworth, Kansas, along with Sherman and another future Civil War general, Daniel McCook. Among his most prominent clients was James H. Lane, whom Ewing successfully defended against a murder charge arising out of confrontation with a fellow abolitionist. Ewing wanted to be a senator like his father but settled for serving as the first chief justice of the Kansas Supreme Court after it gained its statehood.

Like many prominent civilians, Ewing's political connections trumped his lack of military training. He became commander of the Eleventh Kansas

1863-1864: The Destruction of Lawrence and Order No. 11

Infantry Regiment and provided good service at the Battle of Prairie Grove in December 1862. The new commander was met with undiminished violence. On June 6, Quantrill raided Shawneetown, Kansas (near Kansas City). His men killed four civilians and burned several buildings. On June 13, guerrillas robbed civilians near Lexington. On June 17, George Todd and his men ambushed a patrol of the Ninth Kansas Cavalry just outside of Westport, killing fourteen men and wounding four. The cavalry got partial revenge the next day when they attacked a guerrilla camp on the Blue River, killing four. July was the same. Quantrill raided Olathe, Kansas, on July 21. His men killed two civilians, robbed the residents and stole their livestock. Three days later, guerrillas attacked a farm near Harrisonville in Cass County, Missouri. They robbed the stage from Lexington for the fourth time in three months. Federal troops and guerrillas skirmished near Little Santa Fe in eastern Jackson County. On July 26, guerrillas once again held up a stagecoach from Lexington. At the end of July, George Todd led a group of guerrillas in a return to Shawneetown, this time attacking a wagon train. The Ninth Kansas Cavalry rode after them all night, finally catching up with Todd on the Little Blue. But after a skirmish in which the Federals claimed they killed four guerrillas, the rest slipped away in the nearby dense woods. Cole Younger led two attacks on Pleasant Hill on August 10 and 12. Todd went after another wagon train near Kansas City on August 11 and repeated the attack the next day.

Jackson, Cass, Bates, Johnson and Lafayette Counties were all hotbeds of guerrilla activity. Most of the residents were Southern sympathizers. Many

General John Schofield. In cooperation with provisional Missouri governor Hamilton Gamble, Schofield organized and commanded the Enrolled Missouri Militia. He was attacked by Radicals as too lenient on guerrillas and by Conservatives as too harsh. Schofield approved the issuance of Ewing's Order No. 11. After the war, he served as secretary of war and commander of the United States Army. *Library of Congress.*

79

General Thomas Ewing Jr. Ewing was the son of a United States senator and William T. Sherman's brother-in-law. He practiced law in Kansas before the war and was chosen as the first chief justice of the new state's Supreme Court. Although a successful combat leader, he became best known for issuing Order No. 11—a directive that forced between ten and twenty thousand civilians in western Missouri to leave their homes. *Library of Congress*.

had joined the Confederate army or had returned from military service to join guerrilla bands. Federal troops were stationed at various towns and villages throughout the area, primarily in an attempt to protect Kansas from marauding bushwhackers. Outside the military posts, the guerrillas roamed the area at will. The residents provided them food, shelter and intelligence about Federal troop activities.

As the level of violence increased during the summer of 1863, Ewing looked for ways to strike at the guerrilla base. On August 3, he wrote to General Schofield pointing out the difficulties he faced:

> *About two-thirds of the families on the occupied farms* [of the border tier of Missouri counties] *are kin to the guerrillas, and are actively and heartily engaged in feeding, clothing, and sustaining them. The presence of these families is the cause of the presence there of the guerrillas. I can see no prospect of an early and complete end to the war on the border, without a great increase of troops, as long as those families remain there. While they stay there, these men will also stay, if possible. They know they cannot go home and live peaceably because of the fierce feeling against them among the loyal men of the border, who have suffered at their hands…They will, therefore, continue guerrilla war as long as they remain, and will stay as long as possible if their families remain.*

Schofield could not provide more troops to protect western Missouri and eastern Kansas. Under heavy pressure from the War Department, he sent every available man to General Grant for the Vicksburg campaign. Ewing would have to make do with the men he already had—about 1,700—to protect the entire Missouri-Kansas border. He stationed them in twenty company-sized outposts in the hope that they could intercept any guerrilla raiders.

Ewing recommended that the "families of several hundred of the worst of these men" be banished to some place in the South, perhaps Arkansas. He did not want to send any of the families north because he believed the men would follow their families only if they could go to a place where they could be safe. The "least offending" men and their families could be offered terms. Ewing also asked permission to give military escort out of the counties "to such negroes as wish it, and as were slaves of persons engaged in rebellion on or since July 17, 1862."

Although the Federals had banished individuals from time to time, and the Emancipation Proclamation had declared slaves in the Confederate states to be free, Schofield was not about to approve the wholesale deportation of hundreds and freeing slaves in a state that had not seceded without approval from the administration.

Schofield asked Francis Blair Jr. to sound out Lincoln about Ewing's proposal. Blair wrote back that the president's response was an anecdote:

An Irishman once asked for a glass of soda water and remarked at the same time that he would be glad if the Doctor could put a little brandy in it "unbeknownst to him." The inference is that old Abe would be glad if you would dispose of the Guerrillas and would not be sorry to see the negroes set free, if it can be done without his being known in the affair as having instigated it. He will be certain to recognize it as a military necessity.

On August 14, Schofield approved Ewing's plan to deport the families of guerrillas. He cautioned Ewing that "on account of the expense and trouble necessarily attendant upon carrying out this plan, and also the suffering it may cause to children and other comparatively innocent persons, the number to be transported should be as small as possible, and should be confined to those of the worst character." Schofield also approved freeing the slaves of men actively in rebellion, provided that the task should be assigned only to the "most discreet and reliable officers, and you will hold them to a strict account for any abuse of authority or discretion intrusted to them."

Ewing issued General Order Nos. 9 and 10. Number 9 authorized the transport out of Missouri, under military escort and with government-provided rations, of those persons who were slaves and whose masters were engaged in the rebellion. No. 10 directed the Federal troops to escort any loyal persons to Kansas or military stations within Missouri. It further directed the arrest of any persons who aided the guerrillas, including any women not the heads of households, but only those who did so from "disloyal motives," rather than those who were compelled by threats or fears. Finally, Order No. 10 provided: "The wives and children of known guerillas, and also women who are heads of families and are willfully engaged in aiding guerrillas, will be notified…to remove out of this district and out of the State of Missouri forthwith" with their stock, provisions and household goods. If they failed to leave voluntarily, the local officers were directed to forcibly remove them to Kansas City for shipment south. Ewing's order specifically prohibited any soldiers from destroying the civilians' property and prohibited any Kansas troops from entering Missouri without his permission.

Lawrence

In the meantime, William Quantrill gathered a band of nearly four hundred guerrillas to attack the center of Jayhawker activities—Lawrence, Kansas. On August 10, he met with Bill Anderson, Dave Poole and George Todd near Blue Springs, in Jackson County, to urge a raid "on the hotbed of abolitionism in Kansas. All the plunder, or the bulk of it, stolen from Missouri, will be found stowed away in Lawrence. And we can get more revenge and more money than anywhere else." Fletch Taylor had slipped into the town and found it vulnerable to an attack. Some guerrillas were reluctant, pointing out the difficulties in carrying out such a raid—they would have to travel nearly one hundred miles through the cordon General Ewing placed along the border. Quantrill agreed it was "almost a forlorn hope, for if we go, I don't know if anyone of us will get back to tell the story." But, he added, "If you never risk, you never gain."

Even before issuing Order Nos. 9 and 10, General Ewing started his crackdown on the guerrillas' infrastructure. As part of the roundup, Federal soldiers arrested several women, including Bill Anderson's sisters, Josephine, Mary Ellen and Janie, and John McCorkle's sister, Charity McCorkle Kerr. Union troops commandeered a house in Kansas City belonging to Elvira Thomas, the mother-in-law of the artist George Caleb Bingham. Bingham was a general in the Missouri militia and in 1863 was in Jefferson City, having been selected state treasurer.

Anderson's sisters and the other women were jailed in Bingham's former studio, which he added as a third floor to the house. The building was a row house. Thus, the sleepers of the floors served as support for the walls dividing each residence. When cracks began to appear in the walls, the Union provost marshal ordered it inspected. But on August 13, the building collapsed before anything could be done. The inmates were "dreadfully mangled and crushed." Josephine Anderson and four others died. Mary Ellen Anderson was permanently injured, with both of her legs broken, her back injured and her face severely cut.

Exactly why the building collapsed is not known. Some said Federal soldiers negligently removed some of the sleepers supporting the walls for reasons that were never satisfactorily explained. (One rumor said they were trying to get to some prostitutes who were also being held prisoner in the building.) Others pointed out that the added weight of the third story itself could have caused the fall.

The guerrillas were outraged. They were convinced that the Union soldiers deliberately murdered their womenfolk. The incident sealed the decision to attack the town. John McCorkle wrote after the war: "We could stand no more…my God, did we not have enough to make us desperate and thirst for revenge?…[O]ur innocent and beautiful girls had been murdered in a most foul, brutal, savage and damnable manner. We were determined to have revenge."

On August 19, Quantrill led four hundred men from their camp for the march to Lawrence. They camped that night near the Missouri line in northwestern Cass County. The next day, Quantrill led his men into Kansas. Near Aubrey, Kansas, a Federal outpost saw them. The commander, Captain Pike, reported it to the Federal post at Little Santa Fe, Missouri, but the report did not reach headquarters until the following day. No one tried to warn Lawrence or anywhere else in Kansas. The guerrillas marched all night until, at 5:00 a.m., they came upon a hill above the sleeping town.

There was no military guard in Lawrence. There had been rumors of a planned attack on the city, and Ewing stationed a company of troops there. But nothing came of it, and the troops were sent elsewhere. The only soldiers were unarmed colored recruits waiting for assignment and training. The town was defenseless.

Four hundred guerrillas burst into Lawrence at dawn, firing their pistols and yelling. At first some thought it was just "the boys having fun" or someone setting off firecrackers. It soon became apparent that the ruckus was much more deadly. The guerrillas rode into the soldiers' camp, chasing them down as they tried to flee on foot.

Lawrence resident Henry Clarke told of one man on foot, shot more than a dozen times, being chased by a guerrilla on horseback. The bushwhacker fired another bullet into the man. He fell to his knees and held up both hands. "For God's sake, don't murder me, don't murder me," he cried. To Clarke's shock, the horseman shot the man for the fourteenth time, replying, "No quarter for you federal sons of bitches."

The guerrillas rode on toward the Eldridge Hotel, a substantial four-story building in the business district. One witness marveled at their horsemanship and their viciousness:

> *Their horses scarcely seemed to touch the ground, and the riders sat with bodies and arms perfectly free, with revolvers on full cock, shooting at every house and man they passed, and yelling like demons…*[M]*en* [were] *falling dead and wounded, and women and children half dressed,* [were]

The Destruction of Lawrence, Kansas, and the Massacre of Its Inhabitants by Rebel Guerrillas, August 21, 1863, from *Harper's Weekly*, September 5, 1863. *Library of Congress.*

running and screaming—some trying to escape from danger and some rushing to the side of their murdered friends.

Quantrill's men captured several prominent men at the hotel, including the state provost marshal and a correspondent for the *New York Times.* They survived, but many did not. The guerrillas captured eight men, including Ralph Dix, a wagon manufacturer, at Red Leg headquarters in the Johnson House. Dix's wife pleaded with them to spare her husband. One of Quantrill's men said, "I have killed seven Redlegs and I will kill eight more," and shot him in the back.

Jim Lane, the most wanted on Quantrill's death list, managed to escape in his nightshirt and hid in a nearby cornfield. The guerrillas missed the Reverend Hugh Fisher again. He hid in the cellar of his burning house. With his wife's help, Fisher got out of the house unobserved.

Groups of guerrillas systematically went from house to house, calling the men and boys to come out and then killing them. They took money, jewelry and any other goods they could carry away and then burned the homes. At last, the guerrillas returned to the business district, where they set the remaining buildings on fire.

Finally, at 9:00 a.m., Quantrill decided it was time to leave. He left the town in flames and nearly two hundred dead bodies behind. His men, up to that point, had suffered no casualties. One of his men, Larkin Skaggs, robbed and killed nineteen-year-old John Speer Jr. As Skaggs—the last raider to leave—made his way out of town, Speer's brother, fifteen-year-old William, shot him. Another man finished Skaggs off with a bullet to the heart. Skaggs was the only casualty from Quantrill's band during the raid.

Awake for twenty-four hours, many of them drunk and laden with spoils from the raid, Quantrill's men hurried to get away from what was certain to be a frenzied pursuit. That afternoon, a detachment of the Ninth Kansas Cavalry attacked Quantrill's rear guard at Ottawa Creek. The Federals attacked again near dusk at Paola, Kansas, less than fifteen miles from the Missouri state line.

Union troops from Cass County caught up with the guerrillas' rear guard after they crossed into the state. They captured four guerrillas and executed them on the spot. Quantrill's men split up, some hiding in the hills of the Sni-A-Bar River in western Lafayette County, while others headed south along the Grand River.

Jim Lane was furious. He telegraphed Lincoln that he was organizing a Kansas militia to attack Missouri even if he had to fight his way through

The Ruins of Lawrence, Kansas, from *Harper's Weekly*, September 19, 1863. *Library of Congress.*

Union troops to do it. He warned Lincoln that the "result of the massacre at Lawrence has excited feelings among our people which make a collision between them and the military probable. The imbecility and incapacity of Schofield is most deplorable. Our people unanimously demand the removal of Schofield, whose policy has opened Kansas to invasion and butchery." David Anthony, the editor of the *Leavenworth Daily Times*, wrote an editorial on the day following the attack that blamed the disaster on the "know-nothing, do-nothing policy of the general commanding this district [which] has shown his utter incapacity." He also called for Kansans to "depend on ourselves for the defense of our city and state"—in other words, to renew the Jayhawker attacks on western Missouri.

Schofield, however, ordered Ewing to take strong measures to prevent "irresponsible parties" from entering Missouri for retaliation. "Whatever of that is to be done must be by your troops, acting under your own orders." Ewing replied that he would not permit any "unauthorized expeditions into Missouri. No citizens are in now, and none went in except with my troops." The Federal troops, however, showed little mercy for the civilians they found, looting and burning their homes, with little discrimination between Southern and Union sympathizers.

Ewing and Lane met near Cass County. After a bitter argument, they agreed that Ewing would issue the directive deporting Southern sympathizers he had proposed to Schofield a few days earlier. Lane said he would wait to see the results but snapped, "You're a dead dog if you fail to issue the order as agreed between us."

ORDER NO. 11

The destruction of Lawrence forced Ewing and Schofield to take much more drastic action than even that contemplated by Order No. 10. Not just disloyal persons, but everyone, Union sympathizers included, would have to leave their farms.

On August 25, 1863, Ewing issued one of the most famous and controversial orders of the war, General Order No. 11:

All persons living in Jackson, Cass, and Bates Counties, Missouri, and in that part of Vernon included in this district, except those living within 1 mile of the limits of Independence, Hickman Mills, Pleasant Hill, and Harrisonville, and except those in that part of Kaw Township, Jackson

County, north of Brush Creek and west of the Big Blue, are hereby ordered to remove from their present places of residence within fifteen days from the date hereof. Those who, within that time, establish their loyalty to the satisfaction of the commanding officer of the military station nearest their present places of residence will receive from him certificates stating the fact of their loyalty, and the names of the witnesses by whom it can be shown. All who receive such certificates will be permitted to remove to any military station in this district, or to any part of the State of Kansas, except the counties on the eastern border of the State. All others shall remove out of this district. Officers commanding companies and detachments serving in the counties named will see that this paragraph is promptly obeyed.

Ewing wrote Schofield to apologize for not getting his approval first, but he believed it necessary to do something at once to forestall more drastic action by Lane and his cohorts. "The excitement in Kansas is great, and there is (or was before this order) great danger of a raid of citizens for the purpose of destroying the towns along the border. My political enemies are fanning the flames, and wish me for a burnt-offering to satisfy the just passion of the people."

General Halleck asked Schofield whether measures were being taken to prevent the outbreak of internal clashes between Kansans and Missourians and whether Ewing's order "to depopulate certain counties in Missouri has been approved or disapproved by you." Schofield replied on September 2 that he went to Leavenworth to prevent Lane and his followers from attacking Missouri. As for Order No. 11, he took a cautious wait-and-see line, telling Halleck, "I have neither approved nor disapproved General Ewing's order. I think it must be modified, but will not do it until I see him." Schofield later defended the adoption of the order requiring forced removal of thousands of civilians as regrettably necessary because of the "utter impossibility of deciding who were guilty and who were innocent, and the great danger of retaliation by the guerrillas upon those who should remain."

George Caleb Bingham went to Kansas City to personally ask Ewing to relent, but the general was adamant. Bingham was upset at the hardships Order No. 11 would inflict. He was also pained by the death of innocent women in his relative's house—which seemed to have played a role in the viciousness of the attack on Lawrence, even if it was not the cause. As he left the meeting with Ewing, Bingham said, "If you persist in executing that order, I will make you infamous with pen and brush as far as I am able." It was a promise that Bingham would keep.

1863–1864: The Destruction of Lawrence and Order No. 11

With only fifteen days to comply—everyone was supposed to leave the prohibited areas by September 9—many families were caught totally unprepared. They had little or no transport and little idea of where they could go anyway. The result was a chaotic exodus that jammed the roads leading out of the area, mainly to the east and south. Federal officers issued a special order prohibiting those leaving the district due to Order No. 11 from stopping in Clay County, northeast of Jackson County just across the Missouri River.

Most, if not all, of the Union families in the affected counties had already left their homes. In Cass County, for example, about eight hundred Union sympathizers had been driven from their homes to the protection of Union troops stationed at Harrisonville weeks before Order No. 11 was issued. Thus, the effect of the order fell most heavily on the families of Southern soldiers, guerrillas and sympathizers.

Jackson County was hit hard by the evacuation order. Even the Unionists pitied the "poor people, widows and children, who, with little bundles of clothing, are crossing the river to be subsisted by the charities of the people amongst whom they might find shelter."

The experiences of families in Cass County, as recounted by historian Tom Rafiner, were typical.

Martha Moone's husband was serving in the Confederate army. She loaded her six children on to a wagon drawn by oxen and fled to Sedalia. Mary Brookhart's husband was also a Confederate soldier. She decided to take her daughters, ages three and five, to live with her family in Kentucky. After twenty-six days and four hundred miles, they arrived safely.

Elizabeth McFerrin's husband had been shot by Union soldiers at the beginning of 1863. Her oldest son was in the Confederate army. McFerrin had no oxen to pull the family wagon. She rode sixty miles to a relative's home in St. Clair County, borrowed four oxen and brought them back. McFerrin and her six children loaded the wagon and, after many days on the hot, dusty and crowded roads, arrived safely.

John Davidson fought with Sterling Price in 1861 but returned home when the Missouri State Guard disbanded. He and his family traveled to Boone County.

John and Mary Ament were Unionists who lived under Federal protection in Harrisonville, but they wanted to leave too. What wasn't clear was whether Order No. 11 required loyal persons to stay near the designated military posts. On September 3, General Ewing clarified his order to allow Union families to leave as well. The Aments packed and left on September 7.

Ewing issued orders against wanton pillaging, but they were largely ignored. The refugees' difficulties were compounded by sweeps of the area by Union troops, particularly Jayhawkers from Kansas cavalry units. Not only did those fleeing their homes have to share the crowded and dusty roads with a hostile force, but the Kansans attacked many of them before they were even able to leave.

Martin Rice had obtained a loyalty certificate but was preparing to leave as well. On September 6, a squad of Federal cavalry took Rice, his son and his son-in-law prisoners. They also captured one of Rice's neighbors and four others, including a seventy-five-year-old man. All eight were taken to the Union camp, where they were questioned by Federal officers. The officers conferred and told Rice, "You will take your son and travel." Rice had not gone far when he heard several gunshots in quick succession. Although he hoped the Federals were merely shooting game for meals, Rice suspected the worst. A neighbor returned to the camp, where she found the other six men dead, riddled with bullets.

On another occasion, Union soldiers came upon a farm where the owner's wife had just died. They demanded his money, which he said had been sent to Canada for safekeeping. The soldiers scoffed at this story, beat him and searched the house without success. They turned their attention to the coffin. Suspecting that the old man had hidden his money inside, they broke it open, finding only his wife's body. One of the soldiers spied her wedding ring, cut off her finger and took the ring. He told the man's two daughters, "If you want to plant the old lady, drag her out, for we are going to fire the ranch." The daughters pulled their mother's coffin and their injured father out of the burning house.

There were no military posts in Bates County. A few residents took some records to neighboring Henry County to try to preserve some semblance of government, but Bates County itself was cleared of any residents. Vernon County fared no better. Many of its inhabitants had already left before Order No. 11 was issued. Ewing's directive completed the exodus.

By the end of September 1863, the entire countryside south of Kansas City was left in ruins—the former homesteads marked by the remains of chimneys, "Jennison's monuments." Cass, Bates and the northern part of Vernon Counties became known as the Burnt District.

Even hardened guerrilla hunters were shaken by the pitiful sights. Colonel Bazel Lazear, the Union commander at Lexington, wrote his wife it was "heartsickening to see what I have seen since I have been back here. A desolated country and men & women and children, Some of them almost naked. Some on foot and some in old wagons. Oh God."

No one knows the exact numbers of persons who had to leave the area under Order No. 11. Contemporary estimates (and most historians) put the figure at about twenty thousand. Some modern historians say it was more like ten thousand. Whatever the number, it was (as historian Albert Castel pointed out) one of the harshest actions ever taken against American civilians.

PURSUIT OF QUANTRILL
AND THE BAXTER SPRINGS MASSACRE

Within a couple of weeks after the Lawrence raid, Quantrill assembled two hundred of his men for another attack—this time in Jackson County on the steamboats *Mars*, *Marcella* and *Fannie Ogden*. Otherwise, his men hid in the hills of Sni-A-Bar Creek in the eastern part of the county. On October 1, Quantrill moved to Johnson County, where his band grew to four hundred guerrillas, preparatory to riding south to Texas for the winter. They met no resistance when passing through the Burnt District, for there was no one there to resist or impede their march.

Near Baxter Springs, two companies of the Third Wisconsin Cavalry and a company of the Second Kansas Colored Infantry were camped at Fort Blair. Dave Poole, leading Quantrill's advance guard, reported that the Union soldiers were outside the fort eating lunch.

Quantrill ordered Poole to attack them from the south while he attacked them from the north. Poole, however, did not wait for Quantrill. He led his men in a futile charge. The Union soldiers, led by Lieutenant James Pond, fell back inside the sod walls of the fort.

Just at that moment, a wagon train accompanied by about one hundred men from the Third Wisconsin Cavalry and the Fourteenth Kansas Cavalry approached the fort from the north. General James Blunt, the commander of the District of the Frontier, his headquarters brass band and several civilians were riding with them.

Many of Quantrill's men were wearing blue uniforms taken from Union soldiers. Blunt mistook Quantrill's line of battle for an honor guard sent from Fort Baxter to meet him. However, he realized his mistake when the line of men began shooting. Some of the Kansas cavalry broke and ran. The Wisconsin men and the remainder of the Kansans charged

Quantrill's line and fired a volley into it. The firing became general and indiscriminate. Suddenly, about two hundred more guerrillas charged into the mêlée.

Blunt's men fled, but most did not get away. General Blunt also fled, barely escaping with his life. When they finished scattering and killing the cavalry, the guerrillas turned to the wagon train. The band drove their wagon desperately, but after about a half mile, one of the wheels came off. The guerrillas caught up with them. They shot all fourteen members of the band, an artist for Frank Leslie's newspaper, the teamster driving the wagon and a twelve-year-old drummer boy. The guerrillas threw the bodies under the wagon and set it on fire.

The guerrillas captured ten wagons and an ambulance with a loss of four killed and three wounded. The relief column found eighty-five of Blunt's men dead, "nearly all shot through the head, most of them shot from five to seven times each, horribly mangled, charred and blackened by fire." Lieutenant Pond's companies suffered an additional nine dead and ten wounded.

Quantrill left a letter for Blunt, taunting him: "Stop and turn your eyes to Lawrence and Baxter Springs, and see what your amiable policy has brought you to—see what you have done for your fellow soldiers."

Quantrill and his men rode into Texas in triumph. General Price congratulated Quantrill and his "gallant command upon the success attending it." Price wrote Missouri Confederate governor Thomas C. Reynolds that "Colonel Quantrill has now with him some 350 men of that daring and dashing character which has made the name of Quantrill so feared by our enemies, and have aided so much to keep Missouri, though overrun by Federals, identified with the Confederacy."

Aftermath

Ewing partially lifted Order No. 11 in November by allowing persons determined to be "loyal" to return. In January, Ewing's replacement lifted virtually all restrictions on resettlement by permitting anyone who was not "disloyal or unworthy" to return. Many of the bushwhackers' families did come back.

To the extent Order No. 11 played a role in preventing further mass guerrilla attacks on Kansas, it was at least a limited success. Of more importance was the simple fact that the guerrillas left the state in October, and when they returned the next year, they shifted their operations to north central Missouri—in large part to support Sterling Price's invasion. Order No. 11 was politically popular among Kansans but (as Bingham's attitude illustrated) not among Missourians. Confederate general Jo Shelby, who led a raid deep into central Missouri in the fall of 1863, was reported to have said that Ewing's order was "fully justified and...a wise thing to do." In any event, Shelby's men did not pass though the Burnt District on their raid because there were no supplies, no friends and no sympathizers left to rely on.

Chapter 7

1864: The Centralia Massacre

"THERE ARE GUERRILLAS THERE, SURE"

Sergeant Thomas Goodman was anxious to return to his wife, Mary, who he hadn't seen for nearly two years. Goodman, a blacksmith before the war, originally signed up in October 1862 with the Twenty-fifth Missouri Infantry in St. Joseph, Missouri, near his home in Hawleyville, Iowa. His regiment built fortifications at Island No. 10 in southeast Missouri and then spent three months chasing and killing guerrillas in northwest Missouri. In December 1863—in response to General Grant's request for more engineers to help repair and maintain the railroad lines around Nashville—the Twenty-fifth Missouri was consolidated with another regiment to form the First Missouri Engineers. From February to August 1864, Goodman's new regiment built blockhouses and repaired railroad lines from Nashville to Georgia. In August, it joined the main body of Sherman's army for the final battles resulting in the fall of Atlanta.

On September 22, Goodman and many of his friends received "long-promised and eagerly-expected furloughs" to return home. It was a difficult trip. Just thirty-five miles north of Atlanta, the train stopped because Joe Wheeler's Confederate cavalry had torn up a quarter mile of track. The soldiers of the First Missouri Engineers had spent months repairing railroads. They pitched in with the extra incentive of continuing the trip home and replaced the track in four hours. They made it to Louisville via Chattanooga and Nashville under threat of further attacks without incident. Finally, four days after leaving Atlanta, the men arrived in St. Louis.

1864: The Centralia Massacre

Early on the morning of September 27, Goodman crossed the Missouri River to St. Charles to catch the North Missouri Railroad train to Macon, where he would make a connection on the Hannibal & St. Joseph Railroad for the last leg of the trip home. There were rumors swirling around the depot that guerrillas were somewhere out west. A merchant who arrived on an eastbound train also warned of guerrillas, but no one at the railroad seemed concerned. And besides, just the sight of a group of hardened Union soldiers, even though they had no weapons, might scare off the guerrillas.

When the train reached Mexico, there were further rumors of guerrilla activity. Several persons urged the conductor, Richard Overall, not to leave without a military escort. There had been problems earlier. Just three weeks before, guerrillas had attacked a train when it stopped for water at the Young's Creek tank east of Centralia. They stole four carloads of horses and took some soldiers hostage. And another band, reputed to be led by Bloody Bill Anderson, had burned the tiny station at Allen (now Moberly) a couple of days earlier.

Overall decided to continue. He had 125 passengers, including the unarmed soldiers and the railroad's superintendent, on board. If Overall cancelled a trip every time guerrillas were reported on the railroad, he would hardly ever complete one. He gave the engineer, James Clark, the highball, and the train pulled out of Mexico at 11:05 a.m.

As far as Clark was concerned, he was not going to take a chance on being ambushed at the Young's Creek tank. He had enough water to make it to Sturgeon, where there was a blockhouse and Federal troops. He pushed the train to its top speed—nearly forty miles per hour—as it came to the bridge across Young's Creek.

As they approached the water tank, Clark saw a group of men on horses ahead. At first, he thought they were state militia because of their blue coats. But as they drew closer, he could see that he was wrong. Farther ahead, more men were piling railroad ties across the track at the Centralia station. He pulled the throttle wide open and dropped down on the deck of the engine. He hoped that the train's speed would be sufficient to knock the ties aside and allow them to escape to the safety of the Federal garrison at Sturgeon.

Goodman was chatting with a soldier of the First Iowa Cavalry as the train approached Centralia. Now the passengers could see a large body of men milling about the station. Some were on horses, and some were not. Goodman's seatmate took a long look out the window, turned around and yelled, "There are guerrillas there, sure!" What followed next was, as Sergeant Goodman recounted years later, "sickening and atrocious."

United States congressman James S. Rollins was headed to Mexico for the Conservative Party convention. He was running for a second term in the upcoming election. There was no railroad to Columbia, where Rollins lived, so he had to take the stage. The road led north to Centralia and then turned east to become the Mexico Road paralleling the North Missouri Railroad tracks. James H. Waugh, the sheriff of Boone County, was accompanying Rollins to Mexico. The ex-sheriff, John Samuel, and six others were also on the stage.

Rollins was one of the most prominent citizens in the state. He was a successful lawyer who (unusually for the time) actually graduated from a law school. He had been a state legislator and an unsuccessful candidate for governor and the United States Senate before the war. Rollins had his hand in many enterprises; in addition to practicing law, he was a newspaper owner and land speculator. He was also one of the largest slave owners in the state. Rollins did not support Lincoln in the 1860 election (no one did in Boone County; Lincoln only received twelve votes there), but he was hardly in favor of secession. He was a staunch Unionist.

As they approached Centralia, Rollins could see there was some sort of commotion there. Then, about a dozen blue-coated riders came to meet them. But these were not Federal soldiers. They were guerrillas.

That same morning, Major A.V.E. Johnston saw a group of riders heading south. Johnston was a veteran guerrilla hunter. A teacher and part-time preacher in Ralls County before the war, his military career followed an odd path. He first served as an officer in the Missouri State Guard under Sterling Price. He joined the Federal state militia in September 1861. Johnston rose steadily in rank, earning a reputation as an officer who "follows the bushwhackers to fight them on their own ground."

Major A.V.E. Johnston. Johnston was a preacher and teacher before the war. He became an accomplished guerrilla hunter but foolishly led three companies of raw recruits in pursuit of an overwhelming guerrilla force at Centralia. *The State Historical Society of Missouri, Columbia.*

96

1864: The Centralia Massacre

A couple of days earlier, Johnston's battalion had clashed with guerrillas at Santa Fe, in Monroe County. The night before, Johnston had led Companies A, G and H of the Thirty-ninth Missouri Infantry out of Paris to search for guerrillas. Now he found them. He picked up a trail at Middle Grove, a few miles north of Centralia, that led to the southeast toward Young's Creek. Johnston was going to hunt down this band of bushwhackers, too.

The Thirty-ninth was a new regiment that Johnston had helped recruit in Hannibal. Companies A and G were ordered to Paris on September 14. They were joined by Company H on September 22. The outfit was "mounted" infantry. But their mounts were mules and draft animals, "requisitioned" from Southern-sympathizing farmers—useful for transportation only. They were armed with single-shot Enfield rifles, not a cavalryman's carbine. And only the officers had pistols.

The men of the Thirty-ninth could only fight as they would this day—ride to the action, dismount and fight as infantry. The men were not intended or trained to be used as cavalry. Indeed, they were hardly trained at all. Some of Johnston's men had been in the army fewer than two weeks.

Johnston's three companies continued south across the prairie until they hit the North Missouri Railroad. They turned west toward Centralia.

George Todd brought word to the guerrillas that General Sterling Price had invaded Missouri from Arkansas. Price needed their help in diverting Federal troops from St. Louis. Although for most of the summer Bill Anderson had terrorized north central Missouri and successfully eluded Union troops with orders to "exterminate" his band, events turned for the worse in September. On September 23, a Federal patrol ambushed and killed six of Anderson's men and captured one of his "sergeants," Cave Wyatt.

The very next day, Anderson, Todd, Cliff Holtzclaw and about four hundred guerrillas were outside Fayette. Quantrill was there, too, but the others now led his men. Anderson and Todd argued for an attack on the town's garrison. Although these were men of the Ninth Cavalry MSM— among the toughest Union guerrilla fighters—most were on patrol looking for Anderson's gang. Quantrill cautioned against an attack. He pointed out that there was a brick courthouse in the town and the MSM used such buildings as forts. Todd said, "We are going into Fayette no matter what! If you want to come along, all right. If not then you can go back into the woods with the rest of the cowards!" Quantrill left and never went into action in Missouri again.

The Council, from R.P. Bradley, *Outlaws of the Border: A Complete and Authentic History of the Lives of Frank and Jesse James* (1882). With no formal structure, the leaders had to persuade their men to follow them on raids. At councils like these in 1863, Quantrill convinced others to raid Lawrence, and in 1864, he failed to dissuade them from attacking Fayette. *The State Historical Society of Missouri, Columbia.*

The attack was a disaster. As Quantrill predicted, Federal troops took cover in the courthouse. Having failed to take that building, the guerrillas charged to the soldiers' camp on the edge of town. But those men also took cover in log cabins they had built, which were just as impregnable as the courthouse. Anderson and Todd's men had no chance. They were pinned down and "peppered with bullets." Frank James wrote later that he "was mightily scared." The bushwhackers retreated. They lost thirteen dead and thirty wounded; the Ninth Missouri lost two dead. It was a humiliating defeat.

After Fayette, the guerrillas returned to Huntsville. In an act of typical bravado, Anderson sent a messenger to the Union commander, Lieutenant Colonel Denny, demanding his surrender. Unknown to Anderson, two months before he had captured Denny's elderly father, hanged and whipped him and left him for dead. Miraculously, the old man survived, but Denny was ready for revenge. The messenger returned with word from the garrison: "Tell them if they want us to come in and get us." George Todd convinced Anderson not to repeat the Fayette fiasco. So the force moved east. It burned the North Missouri Railroad station at Allen and headed toward Paris. But local sympathizers warned them of the Thirty-ninth Missouri stationed there. They camped at Middle Grove the night of September 25.

The next day, the group moved east to Young's Creek, where a Confederate recruiting party, jittery from its fight with Johnston's men at Santa Fe, mistakenly fired on some of Anderson's men. The recruiters apologized and proposed that they join Anderson. Anderson refused, saying, "Your men are either damned fools or worse, or you would not have fired at us. I don't want anything to do with you."

The guerrilla force, now some 350 to 400 strong, turned south along the creek to the farm of Colonel Middleton G. Singleton, about three miles southeast of Centralia along the wooded banks of Young's Creek. Singleton was a prewar business associate of Congressman Rollins. He and Rollins had laid out the town of Centralia in 1857 in anticipation of the railroad's construction. Unlike Rollins, however, Singleton was an ardent secessionist. He had commanded a battalion of the Missouri State Guard at Lexington. Federal troops had ransacked his home the year before (he complained to Rollins, without apparent effect). Singleton was currently on parole and would be placed on the list for banishment from the state in 1865.

The guerrilla leaders conferred that evening. There were Union troops to the northwest at Sturgeon, to the northeast at Mexico, to the north coming down from Paris and to the southwest at Columbia. At Todd's suggestion, Anderson agreed to take his men into Centralia on the morning of September 27 to see if there was any news of Price.

At mid-morning, Anderson, Archie Clement, Frank and Jesse James and about eighty other men saddled up for the short ride to town.

"WHEN I GIVE THE WORD, POUR HELL INTO THEM"

Until September 27, 1864, Centralia had largely escaped the attacks by either side that other places had suffered. It had no courthouse or Union garrison. It was a community of about two dozen homes, two stores, a schoolhouse, two hotels and a railroad station. It was surrounded by open prairie to the north, south and west. About a mile to the east were the woods lining Young's Creek.

Just before 10:00 a.m. on September 27, a man rushed into town. There were three to four hundred guerrillas camped on Colonel Singleton's place, he said. "Quantrill and Anderson and all of the big bushwhackers are at the head. Hell will be to pay in this country, now!"

Shortly, men in blue coats rode toward town from the southeast—the direction of Singleton's. But they were not Federal troops; they were Bill

Anderson's guerrillas. Anderson's men spread throughout town, forcing their way into every house, demanding food, money and anything else of value. They robbed the stores of virtually everything, including women's and children's clothes.

Anderson bragged to a couple of citizens that Centralia was "a pretty place to fight. If those Feds up at Sturgeon will come down, I will give them a twist today. I don't want to go up there, and I won't, but if they will come down here I'll fight them." Just then, word spread that some of his men had found a barrel of whiskey at the railroad depot.

Anderson followed the rest of his men to the station, where he and the others proceeded to get roaring drunk. The question arose as to how they might bring the whiskey to their fellow guerrillas in camp back at Singleton's. One of them had the bright idea to break open a crate of boots in the freight house and fill each one with whiskey. As they drank, some asked, "How long before that damned train will be here?"

While the guerrillas were celebrating their good fortune, they saw a dust cloud rising from the southwest. It was the Columbia stage. A dozen men rushed to their horses and raced to be the first to rob the unfortunate passengers. The riders surrounded the stage.

"Are there any Federal soldiers in here?"

"None," came the reply.

"Well, get out, all of you."

"What is your name?" they asked Congressman Rollins. "My name is Johnson," Rollins lied, "and I am a minister of the Methodist Church South. I live a few miles south of Columbia." He had been taken prisoner by guerrillas once before—the previous year on a trip home from Jefferson City. That time, he was released through the good graces of a guerrilla leader who recognized him. But Rollins realized that these men, drunken and far wilder than those who had captured him in 1863, would show him no such mercy if they discovered his true identity.

"Out with your pocketbooks," the guerrillas demanded. Some of the passengers protested, "We are Southern men and Confederate sympathizers; you ought not to rob us." The robbers scoffed, "What do we care? Hell's full of all such Southern men. Why ain't you out fightin'?"

The guerrillas proceeded to rifle through the passengers' luggage. One found a shirt belonging to Rollins with his initials written on the hem in indelible ink. Fortunately, the bushwhacker could not read. Rollins talked him out of stealing the shirt by saying that he needed a clean shirt in which to preach on Sunday.

Just then, they heard the sound of a train approaching the depot from the east. The guerrillas hurried back to the station. Rollins and the other passengers took refuge in one of the hotels.

Engineer Clark hoped to crash through the railroad ties piled on the track, but as the train came near town, the guerrillas began to fire their pistols at the train. Bullets thwacked against the sides of the cars and the locomotive cab. Clark's fireman was slightly injured, but the passengers escaped unharmed—for the moment.

Clark couldn't get past the obstacles. The train drew to a halt at the station. Anderson's men burst into the cars and began roughly searching the civilians. Some of the men broke into the express car, where, to their delight, they found over $10,000 in the safe and valises.

But when they entered the car, shouting "Surrender! Surrender!" the guerrillas were taken aback. Soldiers. They had not expected soldiers. "Surrender quietly and you shall be treated as prisoners of war," one cautiously said. One of the Federals, Goodman did not know who, replied, "We can only surrender as we are totally unarmed." Relieved, the guerrillas proceeded to take everything of value from the troops.

Anderson rode up. He ordered the civilians to get off the train and stand by the station; he told the soldiers to line up on the other side of the tracks. Two civilians hesitated, whispering to each other. Anderson shot them dead. The rest quickly complied.

The guerrillas methodically robbed each person—man and woman— of their money, jewelry and watches. One man emptied his pockets at gunpoint. The guerrillas asked him if he had anything else. He said no, but after further threats, he admitted that he had $100 in his boot. The guerrilla took the money and shot him. They also shot another man who tried to hide his watch.

On the other side of the tracks, Anderson ordered the soldiers to strip. One of Goodman's friends and Iowa neighbor, William Barnum, needed help because he was on crutches. The Federals threw their clothes in a pile and stood in their underwear.

Archie Clement asked Anderson, "What are we going to do with these fellows?"

"*Parole* them, of course," Anderson said. "I thought so," Clement laughed. Then he said, "You might pick out two or three and exchange them for Cave, if you can."

"Oh, one will be enough for that," Anderson replied. "Arch, you take charge of the firing party, and, when I give the word, pour hell into them."

Anderson walked to the line of soldiers. They were all hardened veterans. They had hunted guerrillas in Missouri and Arkansas. They knew their fate. "Boys, have you a sergeant in your ranks?" Anderson demanded. No one answered. He repeated the question. Still no answer. Anderson repeated it again, this time his voice rising in anger. "If there be one, let him step aside." Goodman saw the bushwhacker who had taken his jacket with the sergeant's stripes on it start to speak. Almost involuntarily, he came forward. Expecting to die anyway, Goodman could not fathom Anderson's purpose. Two guerrillas took Goodman away from the ranks of his fellows.

Anderson turned to the remaining men. He said:

You Federals, have just killed six of my soldiers, scalped them and left them on the prairie. I am too honorable a man to permit any man to be scalped, but I will show you that I can kill men with as much rapidity and skill as anybody. From this time forward, I ask no quarter, and give none. Every Federal soldier on whom I put my fingers shall die like a dog. If I get into your clutches I expect death. You are all to be killed and sent to hell. That is the way every damned soldier shall be served who falls into my hands.

Some of the soldiers protested that they had fought with Sherman, not against guerrillas. Anderson was unmoved. "I treat you all as one. You are Federals, and Federals scalped my men, and carry their scalps at their saddle bows." Anderson motioned to Clement. The guerrillas opened fire.

In a few seconds, all twenty-three were felled. Goodman watched in horror as the guerrillas methodically went from man to man, shooting each one over and over. All of them, many of them his friends from home, men he had shared hardships and danger with, were shot.

One, however, did not go so easily. Sergeant Valentine Peters, a twenty-four-year-old described by his contemporaries as being of "herculean" proportions, joined the Twenty-fifth Missouri in August 1861. He fought at Lexington, Shiloh and the siege of Corinth. Peters was promoted to sergeant when the Twenty-fifth Missouri became the First Missouri Engineers. Technically, Peters wasn't even a soldier anymore. His three-year enlistment had expired, and he was mustered out of the service in Georgia before leaving for home in Holt County. Peters's war was supposed to be over.

The first fusillade only hit Peters in the shoulder. Despite his wounds, Peters knocked down the guerrilla who shot him and ran to the station on the other side of the tracks. He was able to get under the platform before the guerrillas could finish him off. They set fire to the station. At last, Peters could stand it no more and came out, his underclothes burned away. Infuriated, Anderson's men beat Peters with a club. Then the guerrillas fired twenty shots into his naked body. Incredibly, Peters was still alive. He rose up, cried, "My Lord!" and died.

Goodman watched in horror as the guerrillas went along the line of other bodies, systematically bludgeoning them and shooting the living and the dead. Despite Anderson's proclaimed sensitivities, Clement and several other men took scalps to add to their collection. One of the victims, bleeding from two shots to the face and one to the chest, was dragging his right foot spasmodically back and forth. "He is marking time," Clement joked, and then he shot him.

The other passengers were stunned at the savagery they witnessed. Some wandered about, dazed. Others cried or prayed. Finally, a woman asked Anderson, "May we go to Sturgeon?"

"Go on to hell, for all I care," he replied. With that, Anderson led his men out of town and back to the camp on Young's Creek, whooping, hollering and brandishing the captured boots full of whiskey and their captive, Sergeant Goodman.

"Why, the Fools Are Going to Fight Us On Foot"

Riding from the east, Major Johnston saw the smoke rising from the Centralia depot. As they entered town, the men of the Thirty-ninth Missouri saw the horrific remains of the town's encounter with Bill Anderson—the dead, mutilated bodies, the burning buildings and the rubbish from the looted stores scattered about.

Johnston quizzed the residents about the numbers and location of the guerrillas. Told there were about eighty of them and that they had left to the southeast, Johnston went to the second floor of the hotel to see if there was any sign of the guerrillas. In the distance, he could see a group of perhaps ten or fifteen men riding out of the trees on Young's Creek.

Perhaps skeptical of the previous answers (knowing that nearly everyone living in Centralia was a Southern sympathizer), he once again asked how many guerrillas there were. Thomas Sneed, the hotel's owner, repeated what he had been told earlier. About four hundred were encamped along the creek. Sneed warned, "They all have revolvers and they are better mounted than you are." The major had no intention of engaging Anderson and his men in a cavalry fight. They would take advantage of the longer range of their rifles. Sneed implored, "It is folly to fight them. They are well-trained and desperate men." Major Johnston thought on that for a minute. Then he said, "I will fight them, anyhow."

Johnston left 33 men in Centralia and took the remaining 115 of his command south of town after the guerrillas. He was riding into a classic ambush. The men Johnston saw from the hotel were bait to lead him into the trap. They stopped, fired their revolvers at the Federal troops and rode over a ridge to the east toward Young's Creek. Johnston followed them.

On either side of the ridge were wooded ravines. To the north, John Thrailkill and Tom Todd's men were hidden in the brush. In the southern ravine were George Todd's guerrillas. And at the bottom of the gentle slope to the east were Anderson and Dave Poole's men. Johnston was unwittingly leading his force into a U where they would be surrounded on three sides and outnumbered by three to one.

Johnston crested the hill and saw Anderson's men at the bottom. He ordered his battalion to dismount. In accordance with usual mounted infantry tactics, Johnston left one-fourth of his men behind to hold the horses, while the rest formed a line of battle.

Jesse James at the time of the Battle of Centralia. Note the guerrilla shirt with large pockets and his three revolvers. After the war, Jesse and Frank led a gang of bank and train robbers. Despite the crimes they committed, many Missourians idolized Jesse as a symbol of revenge against an oppressive Radical Republican government—a sentiment that he publicly encouraged. *Library of Congress.*

"Why, the fools are going to fight us on foot!" one of Anderson's men exclaimed. "God help 'em."

Anderson exhorted his men: "Boys, when we charge, break through the line and keep on for their horses. Keep straight on for their horses." He then rode to the front of his men and waved his hat. The charge began.

The guerrillas poured on toward the Union line from three sides. The Thirty-ninth Missouri fired a volley from their muskets that went over the guerrillas' heads. They made the mistake of inexperienced soldiers firing downhill—they aimed far too high. Only one guerrilla was hit—Frank Shepherd, who was reputed to be seven feet tall. He took a round to the head, and his blood and brain matter splattered on Frank James's leg as he charged up the hill. The guerrillas were on Johnston and his men after the first (and only) volley. Some tried to surrender, but the guerrillas were taking no more prisoners that day. The guerrillas had the upper hand in this battle, not only from the surprise of the ambush but also because they were armed with revolvers, which allowed them to shoot the Federals repeatedly before the soldiers could reload their muskets. Only the Union officers had pistols, and even they were overwhelmed by the force and shock of the charge. Johnston died, having fired three shots from his revolver. Frank James claimed that it was his little brother, Jesse, who killed Johnston.

After attacking the troops in Johnston's line of battle, the guerrillas swooped upon the horse holders, nearly wiping them out. Those few who escaped the initial charge fled into Centralia. Lieutenant Thomas Jaynes rode into town shouting, "Get out of here! Get out of here! Every one of you will be killed if you don't." But it was too late. Anderson's men returned to the town and began to hunt down the remainder of the battalion. They searched the houses and outbuildings and killed every Union soldier they found. Only a few of the Thirty-ninth Missouri managed to escape toward Sturgeon. The guerrillas killed 123 of the 148 men who were with Major Johnston that day, including everyone who fought at the battle on Singleton's farm, except for one man. There were no wounded and only one prisoner, Thomas Goodman.

"THE INHUMAN BUTCHER OF CENTRALIA SLEEPS HIS LAST SLEEP"

After hunting down the last of Johnston's men in Centralia, the guerrillas returned to their camp along Young's Creek. The next morning, Anderson, Todd and the rest rode east and south toward the Missouri River. On the same day that the guerrillas decimated Johnston's force south of Centralia, General Sterling Price suffered a crushing defeat in southeastern Missouri. The Federal troops were led by Thomas Ewing, who had been reassigned to St. Louis after being relieved as commander of the District of the Border. Price's much larger force repeatedly attacked Ewing's soldiers in the Union fort at Pilot Knob without success. After nightfall, Ewing blew up the fort and escaped. Price feinted toward St. Louis but turned west to Jefferson City.

Federal troops reached Centralia the evening of the twenty-seventh. They discovered the bodies of the twenty-three soldiers taken off the train and murdered, as well as those of the Thirty-ninth Infantry who were killed in the village. The next day, the Federal troops, led by Lieutenant Colonel Dan Draper, and some Centralia residents went to the battlefield. They discovered yet another ghastly sight. The soldiers reported that they found "a scene of murder and outrage at which the heart sickens." Most of Johnston's men "were beaten over the head, seventeen of them were scalped, and one man had his privates cut off and placed in his mouth. Every man was shot in the head. One man had his nose cut off."

Enrolled Missouri Militia at the blockhouse guarding the North Missouri Railroad trestle over Peruque Creek, just east of O'Fallon in western St. Charles County in 1864. These men are probably members of the Twenty-seventh Regiment EMM, the St. Charles County unit. Note the broad white headbands, which Union commanders ordered the EMM to wear because, lacking uniforms, something was needed to distinguish them from guerrillas. *The St. Charles County Historical Society*.

1864: The Centralia Massacre

Bloody Bill Anderson after being killed by Union militia in October 1864. Note the embroidered "guerrilla shirt" with large pockets for extra ammunition, the plumed broad-brimmed hat and Colt navy pistols. *The State Historical Society of Missouri, Columbia.*

Brigadier General Fisk, the commander of the North Missouri District, increased patrols of the railroad and sent several columns to try to track down the perpetrators of the Centralia bloodbath. They were not successful.

Anderson held Sergeant Goodman prisoner for ten days, much to the amazement of some of his men. On the night of October 7, Goodman managed to slip away from his captors. He worked his way to the Federal post at Fayette. He finally made it back to his home in Hawleyville a week later.

On October 11, Price met with Anderson and Todd at Boonville. Although Price found guerrilla war distasteful, he was desperate for any help he could get from any source. He directed Anderson to return north of the Missouri River and to destroy the North Missouri Railroad trestle over Peruque Creek in western St. Charles County.

Anderson continued his raids, but any military purpose was distinctly secondary. His men, led by Arch Clement, shot five civilians at Danville, including twelve-year-old Ira Chinn, and virtually destroyed the town. They rode to the Danville Female Academy on the edge of town looking for Union soldiers. Some of the students fled into the woods, but others hung a petticoat out the window as a flag of truce and declared they were Southern girls. Clement's men spared the school and galloped east to the home of Unionist state senator Sylvester Baker. The guerrillas rode their horses through the substantial brick house and tried unsuccessfully to set it on fire. After an hour and a half, the guerrillas departed for New Florence and High Hill, where they burned the railroad depots and a water tank. The guerrillas never touched the railroad bridge that was their objective.

By October 21, Anderson had returned west to Glasgow. There, he and his men tortured Benjamin Lewis, a wealthy Unionist, raped one of his teenage slaves and demanded and received a $5,000 ransom from the townsfolk.

But the Federals were closing in. On October 26, Major Samuel P. Cox tracked Anderson down to woods outside Albany. Using the same tactics Anderson had used at Centralia, Cox sent a detachment to lure the guerrillas toward Cox's main body lying in wait. The guerrillas charged to within forty yards of Cox's men. The two sides exchanged heavy fire. Then, Anderson and five of his men charged straight into the Federals. Twenty yards past Cox's line of battle, Anderson fell dead with two pistol balls in his head. Cox took the body to Richmond, where a local photographer took Anderson's picture in his "guerrilla" shirt. Anderson was buried in an unmarked grave.

When Anderson's death became known, one newspaper proclaimed that the "inhuman butcher of Centralia sleeps his last sleep…[the] backbone of guerrillaism in North Missouri" was broken.

Chapter 8

1865: The War Ends, but the Violence Continues

"Oh no," Congressman Rollins must have thought, "not again." For the third time in three years, he was confronted by a band of guerrillas. His stage from Centralia to Columbia was stopped about ten miles short of its destination by four bushwhackers brandishing pistols. Rollins tried to hide his gold watch under the cushion of his seat, but the men found it with little trouble. As he had in Centralia in 1864, Rollins gave the men a false name, claiming to be a farmer living in southern Boone County. The war was over—Lee had surrendered three weeks before—but these men were not finished. There was no pretense that they were supporting the Confederacy anymore. They were simply bandits. Although Rollins did not know it at the time, the robbers were a guerrilla leader named Jim Jackson and three of his men.

While the death of Bill Anderson and Price's defeat did not end "guerrillaism" altogether in Missouri, the level of violence did decrease.

Some guerrillas left the state. William Quantrill, after his falling out with George Todd at Fayette, returned to familiar ground in southeastern Jackson County. He took no part in Price's raid or guerrilla attacks that were supposed to support it. In mid-December 1864, Quantrill and a group of men, including Frank James, decided to leave Missouri for Kentucky. Disguised as Union cavalrymen, they rode southeast into Arkansas, crossed the Mississippi River a few miles north of Memphis and headed north.

Quantrill continued the ruse upon arriving in Kentucky. Three Union soldiers—an officer recruiting for the U.S. Twenty-fifth Colored Infantry, a recently discharged member of the Third Kentucky Cavalry and a member of an Indiana regiment—asked to accompany them. Quantrill agreed. But after traveling a short distance, his men shot two of the soldiers and hanged the other.

Along with local groups of men, Quantrill's band raided several Kentucky towns beginning in February 1865. On May 10, 1865, Federals surprised Quantrill and his men at a farm southeast of Louisville. While trying to escape, Quantrill was shot in the spine, leaving him paralyzed from the neck down. He was taken to Louisville, where he died in a hospital on June 6, 1865.

Frank James escaped the ambush, but he and fifteen others surrendered to Federal authorities on July 26, 1865. John McCorkle, another of Quantrill's men, managed to join a Confederate army unit and was paroled. After his surrender, he got to sleep in a bed—"the first time I had slept all night in a house in three years."

Clifton Holtzclaw left Missouri in March 1865 to wait out the war in Pike County, Illinois. He went to Iowa and Nebraska before returning home to Howard County. He took the oath of allegiance on June 29, 1865. He later moved to Kansas.

Others guerrillas descended into simple banditry. Dave Poole killed two men near Pleasant Hill in Cass County in May 1865. There was no apparent military purpose to the attack.

Arch Clement and about seventy other guerrillas, including Jesse James, spent the winter of 1864–65 in Texas. They returned to Missouri in April and went on a postwar rampage. Clement killed and scalped a member of the militia in early May. A few days later, he led a raid on Holden in western Johnson County, killing a man. The next day, they attacked Kingsville, killing eight men working on the extension of the Pacific Railroad toward Kansas City. After setting homes on fire, they rode into neighboring Lafayette County, where they killed fifteen more. A few days later, Jesse and Clement were riding toward Lexington to surrender (so Jesse claimed) when they ran into a Federal patrol. The soldiers opened fire, and Jesse was shot in the chest. He escaped, but the wound was so severe that he had to be taken to Lexington for treatment. There, he did take the loyalty oath and surrender.

Neither Jesse nor Frank James was heard of in Missouri until December 7, 1869. On that day, two men robbed the Daviess County Savings Association in Gallatin, Missouri, and killed the cashier. Jesse is supposed to have murmured, "Cox, I am bound to have my revenge," before he opened fire in the mistaken belief that his victim was the bank's owner, Samuel P. Cox—the man who killed Bill Anderson.

1865: The War Ends, but the Violence Continues

Jesse and Frank led storied careers as bank and train robbers for the next thirteen years. Jesse was killed by Bob Ford in 1882 while hanging a picture in his home. In 1883, Frank, with the help of newspaperman John N. Edwards, went to Jefferson City and personally surrendered to the Missouri governor. He was tried and acquitted of the Gallatin robbery. Frank died in 1915. His obituary in the *New York Times* noted that he "never was in the penitentiary and never was convicted of any of the charges against him."

The new commander in Missouri, General John Pope, proposed a gradual return of the state to civilian control. Both Washington and Missouri governor Thomas Fletcher, a Republican Radical chosen in the November 1864 elections, agreed. With little fanfare, Pope issued Special Order No. 15 on March 17, 1865, directing provost marshals to confine themselves to military affairs and leave other matters to the civil courts where they were able to resume operation.

As for the guerrillas, they were to be given the chance to surrender, just as regular military troops were. In response to a request for instructions as to what to do about guerrillas, one order read: "Any of these bands that you describe that propose to lay down arms can do so, and the military authorities will take no further action in the case. If they persist in resisting no terms will be granted to them. They are nothing but outlaws. It is too late to surrender after our troops catch them in arms."

One important proviso existed, however. If the civil authorities wanted to try the men for crimes they had committed during the war, the military and its acceptance of their surrender would not stand in the way.

Jim Jackson, Rollins's stagecoach robber, made a show of his surrender. On June 13, he and fourteen of his men rode into Camp Switzler near Columbia. Jackson was in full guerrilla regalia—gray Confederate uniform pants with a yellow stripe down the leg, an elaborate "guerrilla" shirt and four pistols.

Jackson did not last long. After his surrender, he and a member of his gang, William Farley, got more horses and guns. They headed for Illinois but were captured by Audrain County militia. Jackson was identified as the person who murdered a local man during the war. He and Farley both were shot by a firing squad. Rollins found out that one of Jackson's men, William Martin, owned land in Linn County. Although the congressman did not get his watch back, he sued Martin, obtained a judgment and had Martin's land sold to satisfy his loss.

Another guerrilla also faced legal consequences for his wartime actions. Upon returning from California to his home in Cass County, Cole Younger learned that the new sheriff, Reason Judy, had a warrant for his arrest for the murder of Reason's son, John Judy, committed on the way to Olathe in 1862. Younger fled, not to return for three years—this time as part of a gang of outlaws.

John Thrailkill, who had joined forces with Bloody Bill Anderson in September 1864 and played an important role in the ambush of Major A.V.E. Johnston at the Battle of Centralia, went south with Price after his defeat at Westport. He returned briefly to Missouri in the spring of 1865 but soon left for Texas, where he joined General Jo Shelby's men on their way to Mexico. Thrailkill remained in Mexico the rest of his life, where he became a successful businessman. He died in 1895 in Mexico City.

John McCorkle, whose sister was injured in the Kansas City jail collapse in 1863, went to Kentucky with Quantrill. He surrendered in 1865 and was paroled. McCorkle returned to his home in Andrews County, Missouri. He dictated his story to a lawyer, O.S. Barton, and it became one of the best-known guerrilla memoirs, *Three Years With Quantrill: As Told By His Scout*, published in 1914. McCorkle died in 1918 at the age of seventy-nine.

Other guerrillas could not leave a life of violence and met a different fate.

On February 13, 1866, two men walked into the Clay County Savings Association in Liberty, Missouri, northeast of Kansas City. They pulled out pistols and demanded that the owner hand over gold coins, greenbacks and bonds—over $60,000 worth. Another ten men were waiting outside. As the outlaws made their getaway, they fired indiscriminately, killing a nineteen-year-old college student who happened to be on the street. This holdup was the first daylight bank robbery in peacetime. (The guerrillas frequently looted banks during the war.)

The holdup gang was led by Archie Clement and Jim Anderson, Bloody Bill's brother and fellow guerrilla. On April 12, Jim Anderson and another gang member, Isaac Flannery, tried to cash some bonds stolen in the Liberty holdup at a Rocheport bank. Having no success, they left town. Anderson claimed that they were ambushed by state militia shortly afterward. Flannery was killed, but Anderson escaped to a nearby house. Anderson and the house's residents returned for Flannery and found that his gold watch and $2,000 in currency and bonds were gone. There was, however, no sign of a fight. Anderson later left for Texas. There, in 1867, he encountered George Shepherd, a fellow former guerrilla and Flannery's uncle. After sharing drinks one evening, Shepherd asked Anderson to follow him across the street because he wanted to talk privately. Shepherd pulled out a knife and held it to Anderson's throat. He asked Anderson if he had killed Flannery.

1865: The War Ends, but the Violence Continues

John McCorkle (left) and Thomas B. Harris (right). From John McCorkle, *Three Years With Quantrill: As Told by His Scout* (1914). Both McCorkle and Harris accompanied Quantrill to Kentucky, and both survived the war. This photograph was taken in Lexington, Missouri, in the fall of 1864, probably a few days after the Centralia Massacre and Battle. *The State Historical Society of Missouri, Columbia.*

Anderson did not deny it, and Shepherd slit his throat.

Dave Poole, on the other hand, did not leave the state. In early May 1865, he spent several days gathering men hiding out in the brush. He led forty of them into his hometown of Lexington to surrender. Although Poole was not prosecuted for his wartime actions, he did not return immediately to peacetime pursuits.

In mid-October 1866, Poole broke up a meeting of a board that was registering voters for the upcoming election for sheriff. Further violence was averted when one of Poole's relatives, a candidate for the job, persuaded him to go home. Then, on October 30, four men robbed the Alexander Mitchell and Company Bank in Lexington. A posse, led by none other than Dave Poole, chased them but reported that the robbers' horses were too fast. There is little doubt that Poole was in on the heist. But Poole and his posse swore that they "would shoot any man who dare say they had anything to do with the robbery." Eventually, Poole moved to Texas and became a rancher.

These crimes and continued violence, particularly in the former guerrilla strongholds along the Missouri River, prompted Governor Fletcher to call out the militia. "Clay county, Lafayette county, and Callaway county are today worse, if possible, than they were five years ago," complained one paper. The governor decided to send a company of militia under Major Bacon Montgomery to the center of the state's unrest—Lexington.

On December 13, 1866, Arch Clement led twenty-six former guerrillas into Lexington. The governor had decreed that all men should join the militia. Perhaps as a bitter joke, Clement and his men came to town to sign up. Montgomery waited for his chance to take Clement. After completing the papers, most of the guerrillas left town. But Clement decided to have a few drinks at the City Hotel. Montgomery sent four men to arrest him. Three went in the bar to try to get the drop on him. The fourth, however, burst in the door demanding Clement's surrender. Clement drew his gun. In the ensuing fight, the soldiers shot Clement in the chest. He managed to escape the bar, however, and started to ride out of town. As he went past the courthouse, a volley from Montgomery's men brought him down. As he lay on the ground, Clement tried to cock a pistol with his teeth. The soldiers took it away. "I've done what I always said I'd do," Clement said, "die before I'd surrender." Jesse mourned his death the rest of his life. "Arch Clement, one of the noblest boys, and the most promising military boy, [was] murdered in cold blood."

Union soldiers who fought the guerrilla war also returned to civilian life. Thomas Ewing, the architect of Order No. 11, was in Washington, D.C., at the end of the war. He represented accused Lincoln conspirators Dr. Samuel Mudd, Samuel Arnold and Edward Spangler at their trial in 1865.

George Caleb Bingham, Missouri artist, Union general and the owner of the building that collapsed in Kansas City, killing Bloody Bill Anderson's sister just before the Lawrence raid, never forgave Ewing for issuing Order No. 11 and the chaos it caused. He completed two versions of the most famous painting to come out of the war—*Martial Law, or Order No. 11*—in 1868. Bingham described the painting in what his biographer, Paul Nagel, called the most florid terms indicative of how "passion instead of cogent reason dominated the work":

> *The principal group in the foreground of the picture chiefly consists of a venerable patriarch and his family who have just been ejected from their dwelling, which is about to be committed to the flames. A daughter clings to the defiant form of the old man…[A]nother daughter is on her knees before this wretch vainly endeavoring to awaken some emotion of humanity in his callous breast…[A] married man lies weltering in his blood, his young wife bending in agony over his body.*

Ewing, "the brutal assassin," sits on his horse watching a Federal soldier wearing the red leather gaiters of the Kansas Red Legs who just murdered the young man. In the background is "a melancholy procession of dejected and impoverished refugees fleeing from their desolated homes," with columns of smoke rising from them. Bingham had John Sartain make an

1865: The War Ends, but the Violence Continues

Martial Law, or Order No. 11, by George Caleb Bingham. Immediately after Order No. 11 was issued, Bingham went to Kansas City to ask Ewing to rescind it. Ewing refused, and Bingham swore revenge. This 1868 painting was the result. An engraving of the painting was widely distributed and used against Ewing in his campaign for governor of Ohio. *From the Art Collection, The State Historical Society of Missouri, Columbia.*

engraving of the painting. Bingham made numerous speeches denouncing the evils of Radical Republicans. He took one of the paintings with him and sold copies of the prints from the engraving at his speeches.

Ewing returned to his native Ohio to run for Congress. As part of his campaign, he got General Schofield, the commander of the Department of the Missouri who approved Order No. 11, to write a public letter from West Point, where he was then serving as superintendent, justifying the action taken in 1863. Schofield wrote, "Civilization and humanity demanded... [the] prompt suppression [of guerrilla warfare], whatever might be the means necessary to that end." Forced depopulation was, according to him, the only viable alternative to stationing huge numbers of troops—none of whom could be spared because every available man had been sent to assist General Grant in the siege of Vicksburg. "I have never regarded [Order No. 11] as requiring exculpation," Schofield declared. "On the contrary, it was an act of wisdom, courage, and humanity, by which the lives of hundreds of innocent people were saved and a disgraceful conflict brought to a summary close."

115

Bingham responded with a scathing denunciation of Schofield and Ewing. He condemned Order No. 11 as a "heartless atrocity" with "no parallel in modern annals." It allowed Jayhawkers and Red Legs to plunder the affected counties without opposition. "Never was a robbery so stupendous more cunningly devised or successfully accomplished, with less personal risk to the robbers. As an act of purely arbitrary power, directed against a disarmed and defenseless population, it was an exhibition of cowardice in its most odious and repulsive form."

After Bingham's death in 1879, his son carried on the fight against Ewing by distributing copies of the Sartain engraving during Ewing's unsuccessful campaign for governor of Ohio. Ewing lost the election, primarily for internal political reasons, but Order No. 11 certainly kept him on the defensive when it came to his wartime reputation. Later, Ewing moved to New York City to practice law. He died there on January 21, 1896, after being hit by a streetcar while crossing the street.

Like veterans of both sides, former guerrillas came to look on their service with nostalgia. During the war, Unionists condemned guerrillas as "fiends" and "devils." After the war, Confederate apologists portrayed them as "noble outlaws" who fought the good fight for the Lost Cause. Kansas City newspaperman John N. Edwards, a former Confederate officer, painted a favorable picture of men who were driven to desperate acts by the cruelty of Jayhawkers and Union soldiers. Every guerrilla memoir claimed that the author was motivated by revenge and only resorted to violence after he and his family were attacked by barbarous Union troops. They were merely defending their women and children from depredations. At worst, they killed only to avenge personal wrongs. Edwards provided the archetype:

> Reared among the bashful and timid surroundings of agricultural life, he knew nothing of the tiger that was in him until death had been dashed against his eyes in numberless and brutal ways, and until the blood of his own kith and kin had been sprinkled plentifully upon things that his hand touched, and things that entered his daily existence…He lifted the black flag in self-defense and fought as became a free man and a hero.

Frank James defended the killing of Major Johnston's men who were trying to surrender at Centralia in a visit there in 1897. "We did not seek the fight. Johnston foolishly came out to hunt us. Then we killed him and his men. Wouldn't he have killed every one of us if he had the chance? What is war for if it isn't to kill people for a principle?" Former Quantrill lieutenants,

A reunion of Quantrill's raiders, holding his picture. His former guerrillas met from 1898 to 1930. They came to regard themselves as soldiers deserving of the same respect as those who served in the army. As one sympathetic chronicler wrote, they did what they did, "but it was war." *B.J. George Collection, The State Historical Society of Missouri, Columbia.*

such as William Gregg, claimed that even the destruction and killing at Lawrence was justified because it was the center of Jayhawker activity. He argued that "Quantrill and his men only killed soldiers in Kansas."

In the end, former guerrillas felt little remorse over their wartime activities. They organized reunions where they could reminisce with old comrades about their battles, enjoy a picnic and have their photographs taken. The pictures of the guerrillas are similar to the ones taken of Confederate and Union soldiers at their reunions—a group of old men proudly wearing ribbons and displaying a portrait of their leaders.

General William T. Sherman famously said, "Some of you young men think that war is all glamour and glory, but let me tell you boys, it is all hell." The guerrilla war was a special kind of hell. A hell where innocent civilians were gunned down, a hell where wounded soldiers and guerrillas were killed rather than taken prisoner, a hell where the bodies of the fallen were scalped and mutilated. There was no glory in guerrilla war—for either side.

In the end, the guerrillas accomplished little except to terrorize the state. They had no grand strategic objective, let alone any single leader who could develop one. Although the Union progressively wore the guerrillas down, the level of violence increased from year to year, at least until the Confederate defeat became apparent even to the most optimistic Rebel in 1865. By then some of the men could not let go of the bushwhacking life. They were either killed or—like Jesse and Frank James or Cole Younger—became no more than common criminals.

Bibliography

Banasik, Michael E. *Cavaliers of the Brush: Quantrill and His Men.* Iowa City, IA: Camp Pope Bookshop, 2003.

Beilein, Joseph M., Jr. "'The Presence of These Families Is the Cause of the Presence There of the Guerrillas': The Influence of Little Dixie Households on the Civil War in Missouri." Master's thesis, University of Missouri, 2006.

Boman, Dennis K. *Lincoln and Citizens' Rights in Civil War Missouri: Balancing Freedom and Security.* Baton Rouge: Louisiana State University Press, 2011.

Bowman, Frank A. "Appeals in Civil War Missouri." *Marquette Law Review* 93 (2009): 349.

Britton, Wiley. *Memoirs of the Rebellion on the Border, 1863.* Lincoln: University of Nebraska Press, 1993.

Brownlee, Richard S. *Gray Ghosts of the Confederacy: Guerrilla War in the West 1861–1865.* Baton Rouge: Louisiana University Press, pap. ed. 1986.

Carnahan, Burrus M. *Lincoln On Trial: Southern Civilians and the Law of War.* Lexington: University Press of Kentucky, 2010.

Carr, Lucien. *Missouri, A Bone of Contention.* Boston: Houghton Mifflin, 1888.

Castel, Albert. *A Frontier State at War: Kansas, 1861–1865.* Ithaca, NY: Cornell University Press, 1958.

———. *General Sterling Price and the Civil War in the West.* Baton Rouge: Louisiana State University Press, 1968.

———. "Kansas Jayhawking Raids into Western Missouri in 1861." *Missouri Historical Review* 54 (1959): 1.

————. "Order No. 11 and the Civil War on the Border." *Missouri Historical Review* 57 (1963): 357.

Castel, Albert, and Tom Goodrich. *Bloody Bill Anderson: The Short, Savage Life of a Civil War Guerrilla.* Lawrence: University Press of Kansas, 1998.

Connelly, Donald B. *John M. Schofield & The Politics of Generalship.* Chapel Hill: University of North Carolina Press, 2006.

Cozzens, Peter, and Robert I. Girardi, eds. *The Military Memoirs of General John Pope.* Chapel Hill: University of North Carolina Press, 1998.

Fahs, Alice, and Joan Waugh, eds. *The Memory of the Civil War in American Culture.* Chapel Hill: University of North Carolina Press, 2004.

Fellman, Michael. *Inside War: The Guerrilla Conflict in Missouri During the American Civil War.* Oxford, UK: Oxford University Press, 1989.

Fyfer, J. Thomas. *History of Boone County.* St. Louis, MO: Western Historical Company, 1882.

Geiger, Mark W. "Indebtedness and the Origins of Guerrilla Violence in Civil War Missouri." *Journal of Southern History* 75 (2009): 49.

Gilmore, Donald L. *Civil War on the Missouri-Kansas Border.* New York: Pelican Publishing Company, 2008.

Goodman, Thomas. *A Thrilling Record.* Des Moines, IA: Mills & Company Steam Book & Job Printing House, 1868.

Goodrich, Thomas. *Black Flag: Guerrilla Warfare on the Western Border, 1861–1865.* Bloomington: Indiana University Press, pap. ed. 1999.

————. *Bloody Dawn: The Story of the Lawrence Massacre.* Kent, OH: Kent State University Press, 1991.

————. *War to the Knife: Bleeding Kansas 1854–1861.* Lincoln: University of Nebraska Press, 2004.

Harris, Charles F. "Catalyst for Terror: The Collapse of the Women's Prison in Kansas City." *Missouri Historical Review* 89 (1995): 290.

Horwitz, Tony. *Midnight Rising: John Brown and the Raid That Sparked the Civil War.* New York: Henry Holt and Company, 2011.

Leslie, Edward E. *The Devil Knows How to Ride: The True Story of William Clarke Quantrill and His Confederate Raiders.* New York: Random House, 1996.

Marszalek, John F. *Commander of All Lincoln's Armies: A Life of General Henry W. Halleck.* Cambridge, MA: Harvard University Press, 2004.

McCandless, Perry. *A History of Missouri, Volume II, 1820 to 1860.* Columbia: University of Missouri Press, pap. ed., 2000.

Milton, George Fort. *The Eve of Conflict: Stephen A. Douglas and the Needless War.* Boston: Houghton Mifflin, 1934.

Monaghan, Jay. *Civil War on the Western Border: 1854–1865.* Lincoln: University of Nebraska Press, 1984.

Nagel, Paul C. *George Caleb Bingham: Missouri's Famed Painter and Forgotten Politician.* Columbia: University of Missouri Press, 2005.

Neely, Jeremy. *The Border Between Them: Violence and Reconciliation on the Kansas-Missouri Line.* Columbia: University of Missouri Press, 2007.

Neely, Mark E. *The Civil War and the Limits of Destruction.* Cambridge, MA: Harvard University Press, 2007.

———. *The Fate of Liberty: Abraham Lincoln and Civil Liberties.* Oxford, UK: Oxford University Press, 1991.

———. "'Unbeknownst' to Lincoln; a Note on Radical Pacification in Missouri during the Civil War." *Civil War History* 44 (1998): 212.

Nichols, Bruce. *Guerrilla Warfare in Civil War Missouri, 1862.* Jefferson, NC: McFarland & Company, Inc., 2004.

———. *Guerrilla Warfare in Civil War Missouri, Vol. II, 1863.* Jefferson, NC: McFarland & Company, Inc., 2007.

Niepman, Ann D. "General Orders No. 11 and Border Warfare During the Civil War." *Missouri Historical Review* 66 (1972): 185.

Parrish, William A. *A History of Missouri, Volume III, 1860 to 1875.* Columbia: University of Missouri Press, pap. ed., 2001.

Parrish, William E., Charles T. Jones and Lawrence O. Christensen. *Missouri: The Heart of the Nation.* 3rd ed. Wheeling, IL: Harlan Davidson, 2004.

Phillips, Christopher. *Missouri's Confederate: Claiborne Fox Jackson and the Creation of Southern Identity in the Border West.* Columbia: University of Missouri Press, 2000.

Piston, William Garrett, and Thomas P. Sweeney. *Portraits of Conflict: A Photographic History of Missouri in the Civil War.* Fayetteville: University of Arkansas Press, 2009.

Rafiner, Tom A. *Caught Between Two Fires: Cass County, MO., Chaos & Order No. 11 1860-1865.* Bloomington, IN: Xlibris, 2010.

Ross, Kirby, ed. *Autobiography of Samuel S. Hildebrand: The Renowned Missouri Bushwhacker.* Fayetteville: University of Arkansas reprint, 2005; orig. ed. 1871.

Schultz, Duane. *Quantrill's War: The Life and Times of William Clarke Quantrill 1837–1865.* New York: St. Martin's Press, 1996.

Sheridan, Richard B. "From Slavery in Missouri to Freedom in Kansas: The Influx of Black Fugitives and Contrabands into Kansas, 1854–1865." *Kansas History* 12 (1989): 28.

Siddali, Silvana R. *Missouri's War: The Civil War in Documents.* Athens: Ohio University Press, 2009.

Smith, Ronald D. *Thomas Ewing, Jr.: Frontier Lawyer and Civil War General.* Columbia: University of Missouri Press, 2008.
Stevens, Walter B. *A Reporter's Lincoln.* Lincoln: University of Nebraska Press, 1998.
Stiles, T.J. *Jesse James: Last Rebel of the Civil War.* Vintage pap. ed., 2003.
Sutherland, Daniel E. *A Savage Conflict: The Decisive Role of Guerrillas in the American Civil War.* Chapel Hill: University of North Carolina Press, 2009.
The War of the Rebellion: A Compilation of the Official Records of the Union and Confederate Armies. Washington, D.C.: United States Government Printing Office, 1880–1901.
Watts, Dale E. "How Bloody Was Bleeding Kansas? Political Killings in Kansas Territory, 1854–1861." *Kansas History* 18 (1995): 116.
Whites, Leeann. "Forty Shirts and a Wagonload of Wheat: Women, the Domestic Supply Line, and the Civil War on the Western Border." *Journal of the Civil War Era* 1 (2011): 56.
Whites, Leeann, Mary C. Neth and Gary R. Kremer, eds. *Women in Missouri History: In Search of Power and Influence.* Columbia: University of Missouri Press, 2004.
Wolk, Gregory. *Friend and Foe Alike: A Tour Guide to Missouri's Civil War.* Eureka, MO: Monograph Press, LLC, 2010.
Wood, Larry. *Other Noted Guerrillas of the Civil War in Missouri.* Joplin, MO: Hickory Press, 2007.

Index

About the Author

James W. Erwin is a Missouri native. He graduated from Missouri State University with a BA in mathematics. After service in the United States Army, he obtained an MA in history from the University of Missouri and a JD from the University of Missouri Law School. He has practiced law in St. Louis for more than thirty-five years. Mr. Erwin is married to Vicki Berger Erwin. They live in Kirkwood, Missouri.

Visit us at
www.historypress.net
....
This title is also available as an e-book

www.ingramcontent.com/pod-product-compliance
Lightning Source LLC
Chambersburg PA
CBHW060809100426
42813CB00004B/1002